The Five Ways We Grieve

The
Five Ways
We Grieve

*Finding Your Personal Path to Healing
after the Death of a Loved One*

S U S A N   A .   B E R G E R

Trumpeter
Boston & London
2009

Trumpeter Books
An imprint of Shambhala Publications, Inc.
Horticultural Hall
300 Massachusetts Avenue
Boston, Massachusetts 02115
www.shambhala.com

9 8 7 6 5 4 3 2 1

First edition
Printed in the United States of America

∞ This edition is printed on acid-free paper that meets the American National Standards Institute z39.48 Standard.

♻ This book was printed on 30% postconsumer recycled paper. For more information please visit www.shambhala.com.

Distributed in the United States by Random House, Inc., and in Canada by Random House of Canada Ltd

Interior design and composition: Greta D. Sibley & Associates

Library of Congress Cataloging-in-Publication Data

Berger, Susan A.
The five ways we grieve: finding your personal path to healing after the death of a loved one / Susan A. Berger.—1st ed.
p.   cm.
Includes bibliographical references and index.
ISBN 978-1-59030-697-0 (hardcover: alk. paper)
1. Bereavement—Psychological aspects. 2. Death—Psychological aspects. 3. Grief. I. Title.
BF575.G7B476 2009
155.9'37—dc22
2009004270

This book is dedicated to my parents,
Dr. Martin Arnow and Naomi Arnow,
because, as a result of their deaths,
I learned the lesson that Diogenes
so simply expressed:
"Nothing endures but change."

Contents

Acknowledgments   ix

Preface   xiii

Introduction   xvii

1. Loss Changes You Forever   1

2. The Nomad   25

3. The Memorialist   56

4. The Normalizer   83

5. The Activist   112

6. The Seeker   135

7. Transforming Your Grief   161
   Finding Your Personal Path to Healing

8. Hope for the Future   172

   Conclusion   183
   Support for Your Healing

Appendix One

   About the Interviews   187

Appendix Two
　　Resources for Self-Help　191

　　Notes　201
　　Bibliography　211
　　Index　213
　　About the Author　213

Acknowledgments

To all those who have accompanied me on this life-changing journey, I cannot express adequately my deepest appreciation for your support, love, and belief in my ideas and this book, which brings them to realization.

For the participants in my research, the more than sixty amazing people who shared their poignant and profound stories of loss and growth with trust and openness, I learned so much from you and hope that readers of this book benefit as well from your experiences.

To Reverend Rosemary Lloyd, Associate Minister, First Church in Boston, Unitarian Universalist, for her insights about the role of the Church in dealing with loss; Rabbi Karen Landy, Staff Chaplain, Hebrew Senior Life, Roslindale, for providing a contemporary perspective on post-Holocaust God; Thomas A. Welch, Director, Institute of Education and Professional Development, Welch Healthcare and Retirement Group, Norwell, Massachusetts, for his wisdom and support in formulating my understanding of worldview.

To my wonderful agent, Janet Rosen at Sheree Bykofsky Associates in New York, who believed that my book would "help lots of people" and who tenaciously pursued many publishers until she found it the perfect home.

To my editor, Emily Bower, at Shambhala Publications, who believed in the message my book would bring to readers and the contribution it would make to the field of bereavement, as well as the assistant editor, Ben Gleason, and the copy editor, Susan Cohan, whose contributions made it a better book.

To Grace Talusan, my magnificent, supportive, thoughtful editor, who helped position my book proposal with my sample chapters, offered valuable editing and input as I wrote various chapters, and always seemed to know what I needed to write and how to help me do so.

To Michelle Silver and Grub Street Writers, who got me started on my writing journey, as well as editors Emily Miller and especially Gail McMeekin, who fine-tuned my book proposal for submission.

To my many colleagues through the past nine years, including Lisa Barstow, who had confidence in me when I lacked it in myself, provided input and feedback, read very early drafts, and offered help whenever requested.

To my dear friends Natalie Camper, Cynthia and Steve Drysdale, Barbara Feldman, Corey and Marvin Freedman, Simeon Goldstein, Sandy Katz, Nancy Kaufman, Holly Korda, Selma Mirsky, Ginny O'Brien, Marjorie Share, and Rae Simpson, for sharing my joys and comforting me in my pain. My special gratitude to Maia Greco, who lent her keen eye for detail to the proof.

To my brother Eric Arnow, who has inspired me with his wisdom; my cousins Layne and Jeff Lepes; Rachel Finnin; Emily and David Ma; Judy and Skip Livingston; Lenore Arnow; and Stephen and Sherry Schlakman, who are dear to me for being my family.

To Uncle Sidney and Aunt Charlotte Grodberg, who have always been there for me.

To my daughter and son-in-law, Rachel and Art Weeks, who have given me Jason, my hope for the future.

Preface

THIS BOOK is a personal mission and an opportunity to link my areas of professional interest with my personal experience. Having lost both parents at an early age, I have spent much of my life asking questions about why this happened, pondering what effect their deaths had on me and my family, and considering what contributions I could make to those who have had similar experiences or those who work with people who have lost loved ones. As I matured, I developed a perspective on the impact of these losses on my life— the large and small ways my life changed as a result. These ways included the choices I made, the priorities and values I embraced, and the people I chose as my friends. My professional development was clearly guided by my own loss experiences.

Many of us have begun to examine the meaningfulness of our own lives in recent years. Perhaps this contemplation was spurred by the sudden, violent, and traumatic tragedy of September 11, 2001. Perhaps it has been inspired by the public chronicles of dying people such as Morrie Schwartz from *Tuesdays with Morrie*,[1] and more recently Randy Pausch, whose book *The Last Lecture*[2] urged us to appreciate joy and love as life's greatest gifts. Such events cause us to reflect on the grief and despair that each of us feels when we lose a loved one. Although we assume grief has psychological effects, at least for a period of time, most people are unaware that our losses affect us forever, since they cause us to see the world and ourselves differently. The task of discovering "Who am I now?" and finding our own path to healing represents one of the greatest challenges of the grieving process.

Losing a loved one is a difficult topic for most of us, particularly in American society. We Americans tend to deny the reality of death. Our relatively young country, with its history and tradition of hope and opportunity, is populated with generations of citizens from all over the world who have come here to take part in the future. Unlike the more ancient civilizations of Asia, Africa, or Central America, we do not view the past as our teacher. We worship youth, beauty, and the power derived from them. We place less value on the old ways or the wisdom that has been acquired through lifetimes or centuries of experience.

Even though all of us will die, acknowledging the inevitability of death flies in the face of our deep-seated belief in our ability to overcome adversity. Creating our own destiny is our cultural heritage. The individual freedom Americans enjoy provides us with many chances to start over, to select new jobs, new homes, and new relationships. Empowered by such opportunities, we can suppress thoughts of suffering and bury memories that cause us emotional pain. Even if we have lost a loved one and experienced grief, we are expected to recover quickly and move on with our lives.

This belief was in part supported by the groundbreaking research of Elisabeth Kübler-Ross in the mid-twentieth century. She identified five stages of grief—denial, anger, bargaining, depression, and acceptance—that dying individuals experience.[3] This theory of grieving was adopted as the accepted approach for helping the dying as well as their survivors through the grieving process. Since then, however, bereavement researchers and clinicians have discovered that this theory falls short of addressing the unique needs of survivors of loss. An excerpt from a poem by Linda Pastan poignantly illustrates this error:

> . . . Denial was first.
> . . . Anger seemed more familiar.
> . . . Bargaining. What can I exchange for you?
> . . . Depression came puffing up.
> . . . Acceptance. I finally reach it.
> But something is wrong.
> Grief is a circular staircase.
> I have lost you.[4]

The five stages of grief do not ultimately offer bereaved individuals comfort or assistance. Survivors must go on. But they follow a different trajectory toward healing, one that involves not just shock and denial but also confusion, disorganization, and despair before they can reorganize their lives. This process is not linear, as the stages imply, nor is it generic. Our knowledge of grieving and healing informs us that recuperating from significant loss is like any other healing process: it occurs over time and requires considerable energy. Each person heals differently.

For those of us who have experienced death in our lives, we realize that the environment in which we live is no longer the same. We suffer anguish and turmoil through which we must nevertheless rebuild our lives. This book's message is one of hope and encouragement for finding meaning from your losses and discovering yourself as a changed person.

With greater awareness and understanding of the long-term impact of loss, I believe that all who have lost loved ones can find new, fulfilling, and purposeful lives. I hope this book will help you find yours.

A NOTE ABOUT THE INTERVIEWS

All of the people I interviewed for this book have given me permission to use their stories. Most of their names and details of their experiences have been changed. Several people preferred that their real names be kept. I have respected their preferences, but have not differentiated them.

Introduction

FIFTY is not just a number to me.

Just shy of fifty, my cousin Helen lost a long battle with colon cancer. That same year my lifelong friend Edda, almost fifty, died of a virulent brain tumor just ten months after diagnosis. Both my parents had died young, my father at age thirty-five and my mother just nine days short of her fiftieth birthday.

Later that year when I turned fifty, I was very unhappy. My career began to falter as I worked a series of unsatisfying jobs. I lived a nomadic existence and was unfocused, depressed, with no sense of direction. I couldn't decide what I wanted to do with the rest of my life. Helping others improve the quality of their lives had always been a high priority in my life, but I found it frightening that I was unable to do the same for myself. I was stuck.

And then suddenly I understood: I hadn't expected to reach my fiftieth birthday.

No wonder I was lost; I had made no plans beyond fifty because I didn't think I'd still be alive.

In an attempt to understand what was happening to me, I began a process of self-examination. I read about grief and loss in the works of great thinkers and writers, from Freud's "Mourning and Melancholia" to *Man's Search for Meaning*, by Holocaust survivor Viktor Frankl.[1] I read current research on loss and bereavement. I thought about the reality of mortality, the painful truth about love and death. I realized that losing loved ones and dealing with grief is a lifelong process, something that unfolds and impacts your life long after the acute symptoms of grieving subside.

After this process of self-discovery, I felt the need to connect with others who had lost loved ones. In our society, we work very hard to deny the existence of death. We color our hair and relax our wrinkled foreheads as if hiding the signs of aging will negate the inevitability of death.

When someone has lost a loved one, we tend to withdraw and stay away, telling ourselves not to bother the bereaved. Meanwhile, the bereaved feel isolated and alone. We say, "I'm sorry for your loss," and not much else, as if it were impolite to talk about death or even bring it up much beyond the immediate aftermath of the loss.

Since I was interested in how significant losses affected other people, however, I tentatively began to broach the subject with bereaved friends and acquaintances. When I questioned these survivors, I was very surprised to discover that they were hungry to share their stories.

I asked survivors the following questions:

- Did the significant loss force you to think about your own mortality?
- Did you feel suddenly vulnerable to death yourself?
- Did you struggle for many years after the death to build confidence and find a sense of purpose?
- Does the loss continue to affect you?

- Did the loss influence how you see yourself in relation to others and the world?
- Did the loss transform your perspective on life and where you fit in?
- Did the loss give you as a survivor a sense of identity and purpose you had not recognized before?
- Did the loss prompt you to do something you would otherwise never have done?

My project brought unexpected results. For the first time in more than thirty years, my brother, who was living as a Zen Buddhist in Asia, shared with me his feelings about our parents' deaths and his experience of those deaths. We talked together for the first time about how those losses had affected our lives. Friends of friends and people in extended networks began contacting me, interested in talking about their experiences with the death of loved ones. Long after the funerals were over and what society regards as an appropriate grieving time had passed, survivors wanted to share how significant deaths had shaped the way they lived.

Through this work, I learned that those of us who have experienced the loss of a loved one shared certain sensibilities. Contrary to social expectations, we hadn't merely recovered from our losses and resumed the lives we had been living. I found that others who had experienced losses similar to mine compared their life span to that of the parent they had lost. We all felt a heightened sense of our own mortality. We all experienced episodes of grief and painful images, triggered by birthdays, anniversaries, holidays, and other associations with our loved one. No matter whom we had lost—a parent, sibling, spouse, or lover—no matter whether this loss had occurred five years ago or forty, we acknowledged that our losses had significantly changed our lives.

Though I found a measure of personal solace in the wisdom I had gained, I realized others might appreciate the shared knowledge and wisdom as well. This is when I decided to write this book, to compile the stories of long-term loss, to identify themes among the stories, and to explore the ways that people create meaning from loss. As survivors of loss, each of us changes. We are not—and cannot be—exactly as we were before. We adapt to our new life situation, personally and socially. Our view of the world changes; our priorities, and sometimes our values, change.

During my doctoral studies at Harvard, I examined the works of researchers and scholars and was trained to find themes and make connections. As I began collecting the stories of more than sixty survivors of significant loss, I started to see patterns. When people experience the loss of a loved one, they consciously or unconsciously develop a new identity based on their changed circumstances. What emerged from this work was my theory that there are five "identity types"—which I have called nomad, memorialist, normalizer, activist, and seeker—each of which represents a different way of creating meaning from the loss of a loved one in order to give the survivor's life a new purpose.

In this book, I discuss how the psychological, social, and spiritual factors I examined in my research contribute to the formation of these identity types. I describe and explore each of the identity types, including its advantages and disadvantages, its strengths and weaknesses, in order to help you understand the identity you have chosen in response to the loss of your loved one. I also suggest strategies you can use to improve the quality of your life and promote healing, either by working within your present identity type or by working toward adopting another identity type that you might find more fulfilling.

THE FIVE IDENTITY TYPES

1. *Nomads* are characterized by a range of emotions, including denial, anger, and confusion about what to do with their lives. Nomads have not yet resolved their grief. They don't often understand how their loss has affected their lives.

The remaining four types have chosen their personal path to healing

2. *Memorialists* are committed to preserving the memory of their loved ones by creating concrete memorials and rituals to honor them. These range from buildings, art, gardens, poems, and songs to foundations in their loved one's name.

3. *Normalizers* place primary emphasis on their family, friends, and community. They are committed to creating or re-creating them because of their sense of having lost family, friends, and community, as well as the lifestyle that accompanies them, when their loved one died.

4. *Activists* create meaning from their loss by contributing to the quality of life of others through activities or careers that give them a purpose in life. Their main focus is on education and on helping other people who are dealing with the issues that caused their loved one's death, such as violence, a terminal or sudden illness, or social problems.

5. *Seekers* look outward to the universe and ask existential questions about their relationship to others and the world. They tend to adopt religious, philosophical, or spiritual beliefs to create meaning in their lives and provide a sense of belonging that they either never had or lost when their loved one died.

LOSS AFFECTS US ALL

The loss of a loved one affects us forever. Significant loss changes our sense of who we are and our place in the world.

At the same time, significant loss can be an opportunity to create positive change in our lives and in the world. Look at what John Walsh, host of the television program *America's Most Wanted*, has achieved in helping people after the tragic murder of his young son, Adam.

Each of us who has suffered loss can transform our experience into an opportunity for growth. But in order to do so, we must first come to terms with our grief. Then we can work toward creating an identity and a life that integrate our lost loved one and our experience of loss in a positive way. We can find new meaning and purpose for our lives.

If you have ever loved someone, you face the possibility of someday losing that person. This is the risk of loving, but to me, loving is the only experience worth anything in this world.

HOW THIS BOOK WORKS

This book can help you understand how loss has affected your life and shaped you into the person you now are. This understanding will allow you to examine your motivations for past decisions and choices and identify your strengths and weaknesses. It will also help you pursue ways to resolve unfinished grieving and heal from your loss.

First, you must accept the basic premise of this book: after someone you love dies, the most daunting task you face is rebuilding your life and finding a new identity. Because you defined yourself in relation to the person who died, you must, as bereavement expert Thomas Attig explains, "relearn the world,"[2] including your relationship with the deceased, your friends and family, and yourself as well. This task of redefining yourself, of finding a new identity after the death of your loved one, is a process that begins after the person has died and continues throughout your lifetime. Therefore, the better you understand yourself and how your loss has affected your life, the more able you will be to meet the challenges of being a survivor and having a satisfying and purposeful life.

To gain the greatest benefit from this book, start at the beginning—even if you are tempted to read first about the different identity types. Why? Because the identity types are based on information in the early chapters. The introduction describes my own experience and lays the groundwork for understanding how and why I concluded that finding a new and meaningful identity is critical to adapting successfully to a changed life—a life without your loved one. Chapter 1 describes how loss changes you forever—how your *worldview* is shaped, and how this is likely to change your identity, your sense of who you are. I introduce my idea of "the four pillars of identity," and show you how they can help you find meaning from your loss, and a new fulfilling purpose in life.

I then go into detail about the five identity types: nomad (chapter 2), memorialist (chapter 3), normalizer (chapter 4), activist (chapter 5), and seeker (chapter 6). Each of these chapters begins with a definition of the identity, including a typical example for the type, drawn from a well-known event, a published article, or a film. Several key people I interviewed tell their stories of loss, and I examine why they represent the particular identity type. Their stories, often powerful, always poignant, will illustrate the advantages and disadvantages of that identity type. Theory or concepts that support or shed light on issues relevant to the identity type are woven throughout the discussion, and I propose strategies for maximizing the potential of each identity. Each of these chapters ends with questions for you to answer to help you determine whether this identity best reflects the person you have become since your loss or want to be as you attempt to heal and move forward with life.

Chapter 7 guides you through five questions that can help you identify your personal path to healing. These questions, based on what I call the four pillars of identity (discussed in chapter 1), will allow you to examine whether and how your worldview changed after you experienced your loss. Chapter 7 also enables you to evaluate your present identity type (which you discovered in the identity type chapters), examine any "identity hang-ups" that may be preventing you from resolving your grief, and explore many suggestions for helping you heal.

Chapter 8 is a call for hope and action, in which I discuss how this book offers hope for all of you who have been affected by the death of a loved one but have not yet fully understood how this loss has influenced your life and your identity. I challenge you to evaluate your current life and your level of success in creating meaning and purpose as a result of your loss. This new insight will allow you to decide whether your current identity type suits you or whether you would prefer to work toward adopting a different identity that could further your healing.

The conclusion reminds you that you are not alone. Even if you have no family or friends, or you just feel isolated, your community offers numerous sources of support for survivors of every stripe. This chapter discusses the types of resources available—such as nonprofit organizations, support groups, libraries, churches and synagogues, and colleges and universities—and what they can offer you. An array of bereavement resources also exists at the state and national level to help you deal with the issues of your loss.

After you have read this book, I hope you will see it as a tool that you can use and return to again and again as you confront issues related to your present loss and subsequent losses throughout your life. Whether you are a bereaved individual, a professional working with the bereaved, a caregiver, or a volunteer helping others deal with their losses, this book will help you better understand the *long-term impact of loss* and more fully appreciate the uniqueness of each individual's struggle to adapt to loss and find a new and fulfilling self.

The Five Ways We Grieve

One

Loss Changes You Forever

I WAS ELEVEN YEARS OLD when my father died. It had
been a long, painful illness, during which he gradually lost
strength, functioning, and, ultimately, the will to live. It was
1956, and at that time I was made to feel that illness was
shameful. My father began taking weekend "fishing trips,"
which I later learned were clandestine admissions to a Boston
hospital for experimental treatments. I watched my father
grow weaker and weaker: he reduced his work schedule to
half days, then began using a walker, then became bedridden. While I was lying in bed, when my parents thought I
was sleeping, I would hear my mother whisper comforting
words to my father as she bathed him, wiping the wash-
cloth gently over his blotched skin and his welts and sores.
Again and again, my father would cry, "I want to die." He
was thirty-five years old.

On a typically gray day in December 1956, my eight-year-
old brother and I walked home from school. We arrived to
find my mother and my aunt huddled together on the front
porch, their coats pulled tightly around themselves against
the cold. My mother said it. "Daddy died." I was eleven years
old, but I had known this was coming. I was relieved that I

had stopped to say good-bye to my father before leaving for school that morning.

Although we all did our best to continue living, an invisible cloud hovered over us for the following nine years during which my mother, brother, and I lived together. My father had been a prominent dentist, and I watched enviously as the sons and daughters of his colleagues went to private schools, took family vacations, and lived in homes in elite suburban neighborhoods. We remained in a wood-frame, three-decker building in the city, with my aunt, uncle, and two cousins living on the second floor and my maternal grandparents on the top.

My mother worked full-time as an elementary school teacher and held two part-time jobs in the summer and on weekends. Long before there was the term *latchkey kid*, my brother and I spent our life outside of school in an apartment with no adults. We realized we were different, especially when all the other families we knew and watched on *Father Knows Best* and *Ozzie and Harriet* were two-parent families. With only my brother, who was also grieving, for company, I felt isolated. I recently learned that my brother was furious with my mother for years afterward for abandoning us to her three jobs rather than spending time with us.

Although we didn't want to admit it, that devastating December day forced all of us to change. My mother became a widow. My brother and I had to start finding our way through life without a father. Even now, when I think about the ways our lives have unfolded in the decades that have passed since his death, it still astounds me how profound an impact losing him has had on our lives.

My story illustrates how my own life and that of my family changed from the moment of my father's death. Not only did we lose his physical presence in our daily lives, but we also suffered an intangible yet deeply felt symbolic loss: our future as a family. We lost the hopes and dreams that we associated with him. No more plans. No more happy memories to create together. Life as we knew it had ended.

These physical and symbolic losses influenced every part of our lives, tinted the lens through which we viewed the world, and changed the way we lived. The changes in our world also led to changes in how we viewed ourselves and how others viewed us. We lost our identities, because when we lost my father, we lost parts of ourselves—especially the parts that were defined by our relationship with him.

OLD IDENTITY TO NEW IDENTITY

When we survive the loss of a loved one, we are forever changed. We are not exactly the same as we were before, nor could we be. We find ways to adapt personally and socially to our altered life situation; our worldview shifts; our values sometimes change, as do our priorities. Whether we are aware of doing so or not, we develop a new identity based on these changes—an identity that reflects how we have created meaning from our loss and that can give our lives new purpose.

I believe that the process of evolving from our old identity to our new one goes something like this: After loss occurs, we begin to make choices, consciously and unconsciously, that reflect this life change. These shifts in previous patterns include a heightened awareness of life and death, a reevaluation of our values and priorities about what is truly important in our lives, and modified perceptions about our existence.

For example, the sudden death of a spouse or sibling forces you to confront your own mortality. You are faced with the reality that life is fragile and short, that it can be taken away or altered quite dramatically, quite suddenly. This realization can be a wake-up call to live a better life, or it can be a deep hole that you step into and can't quite lift yourself out of.

We integrate these new beliefs (for example, that life is short) into our lives as a way of creating meaning and new intentions for our lives. Through this process, we metamorphose into a reinvented "self" with an identity that can lead us to more (or less) fulfillment and an enhanced (or diminished) sense of purpose for our lives.

There are numerous informative books designed to help people understand what the grieving process is and how those who have been left behind can work through their pain and move on with their lives. In my view, however, none of these books adequately addresses the significant questions that I faced as a survivor of loss: Who am I now? What choices do I have? What is now the purpose of my life?

The Five Ways We Grieve is not just another book about the grieving process, nor is it just another book about the anguish of losing a loved one, however important these topics are. Rather, it offers guidance in the process of forming a new identity and mission in your life after a major loss.

This book's purpose is to examine the challenge of finding identity and meaning after your loved one is gone and help you explore the possibility of carving out a new way of being in the world. It provides many poignant and powerful examples of how others have accomplished this. It can inspire you to do the same and help you successfully adapt, heal, and create new meaning for your life.

THE IDENTITY TYPES

Each person who experiences a loss through death is unique. Yet my research suggests that most survivors of loss respond in similar patterns to form a new identity. The five patterns that I refer to as the survivors' identity types are: the nomad, the memorialist, the normalizer, the activist, and the seeker. Although these identity types were created with the ultimate loss—death of a loved one—in mind, they are useful for anyone who has experienced any significant loss that impacts his or her identity. These identity types can empower you as a survivor of loss since they offer different perspectives for redefining your life.

1. *Nomads* are those who have not yet resolved their grief in a way that allows them to move on with life and form a satisfying new identity. Whether their loss occurred three years ago or thirty, nomads remain adrift or confused. They do not have a clear sense of themselves or their relationship to the world. They make inappropriate choices for their lives and lack an internal compass to guide them. These people have not had the support necessary to acknowledge their grief and go through all the complex yet necessary steps of the grieving process. As a result, nomads have no anchor to provide them with security or stability. They lack a clear identity. The nomads' challenge is to find an identity that will help them heal from their loss and align with a particular purpose and perspective that suits them.

2. *Memorialists* are people whose main goal is to honor their loved one by creating concrete objects or rituals that perpetuate his or her memory. They need to maintain connection with their loved one by integrating the person into their life through these activities. Whether the practices are determined by culture, religion, ethnicity, or individual beliefs, memorialists have the most powerful need of all of the identities to honor their loved one with tangible tributes that bear the loved one's name. I found that this is one of the most commonly adopted identities for survivors of loss.

3. *Normalizers* appreciate that life is finite. They work to create the kind of life they either lost or wished they had. Although they are guided by their loss, their main concern is the quality of their present and future life—for themselves and their family. Their values and priorities reflect their desire for "normalcy" and a good life. I have found normalizers who create new families through adoption after tragic loss of children, spouses who love being married and remarry to recapture that love and security, and adults who replicate their childhood dreams through their own families.

4. *Activists* have an increased awareness of the time-limited nature of existence along with a desire to make a difference. Hungry for intense and varied life experiences, they are oriented primarily toward the future, striving to create meaning through the positive impact they can have on people and the world. Their values and priorities are directed toward making this world a better place for all people, improving the quality of life, and sharing their hearts and minds with others. Activists have been mobilized by their own losses to create social justice for others, to advocate for social change, to participate in activities that raise funds to combat disease, to write, to educate, and to empower others by their creative talents.

5. *Seekers* experience their loss as a catalyst for philosophical inquiry into the meaning of life. Although seekers are less prevalent than the other identity types, they tend to believe that humans are intended to fulfill some specific purpose in life, often acknowledging that this earthly life can be transcended by other forms of reality. Seekers value connection with one another, the natural world, and the divine. They explore both the range of human experience on this earth and the universe with all its mystery. Seekers find comfort in

belonging to groups or sharing lifestyles with others who hold similar spiritual beliefs.

THE IMPACT OF LOSS AND THE IDENTITY TYPES

Since the impact of loss endures throughout our lifetime, we may shift from one identity type to another as we experience various events, memories, and life passages. Sometimes we adapt consciously, but often we are unaware of how our loss affects our choices and actions. Although unconscious beliefs may disrupt our sense of ourselves, I maintain that each of us adopts a *dominant* identity that defines us throughout our life.

My own experience with the identity types provides a useful example. I was a nomad until I confronted a strongly held unconscious belief: because neither my father nor my mother had lived past the age of fifty, I believed I would die before I turned fifty. Now that I've spent a few years working with the identity types, I've transformed my dominant identity into that of an activist. Writing this book to reach out to others struggling with loss—that is my way of transforming my loss into a productive action that may benefit a larger community.

HOW OUR WORLDVIEW CHANGES AFTER LOSS

From the moment we are born, we search for safety and security and learn to trust others in our uncertain postbirth world. Harvard psychoanalyst Erik Erikson, noted for his work on human development, informed us that an infant's first developmental task is to form trust in his or her environment, and particularly his or her parents. After all, our parents' biological purpose is to love us unequivocally, provide for all our physical needs, protect us from harm, and express warmth and affection that convey to us that we are loved and worthy of their love. As a result, most of us grow up with a well-integrated sense that, as Ronnie Janoff-Bulman, a researcher on the effects of loss and trauma, says, "the world is benevolent, the world is meaningful, [and] the self is worthy." What she means is that most of us believe we live in a world where people are "generally good, kind, helpful, and caring," and events yield predominately "positive outcomes and good fortune." People consider themselves good, capable, and moral, resulting in a sense of security, trust, and invulnerability deeply embedded in our psyche.[1]

Yet, when we lose someone significant in our lives, these assumptions often fall apart. As Professor Robert Neimeyer, a major leader in bereavement research and practice, suggests, our life's narrative is interrupted. After loss, the world in which we live is immediately and irrevocably changed. All the building blocks of the platform we have so carefully and thoughtfully constructed tumble down in a heap. Like Humpty Dumpty, we have fallen off the wall, broken into millions of pieces that cannot be put together again. This nursery rhyme tells the truth: We can never be reassembled in exactly the same way. We are forever changed by our loss.

Gradually over time, and perhaps without fully realizing it, everyone who experiences a significant loss goes through a complex transformation. Just as our external world changes, so does our inner world. Our identity is revised by a combination of shifts in how we see the world, what we determine is important in life, and how we create meaning from our loss.

Over the course of my life since my father's death, these shifts have blended together to form a worldview through which I see my surroundings and my place in the world. This worldview incorporates my beliefs and values, based on my knowledge, ideas, and experience. My colleague Tom Welch, a Jesuit priest and an early leader in the field of death, dying, and hospice, reinforced my own thinking about the significance of "worldview" as a means of understanding ourselves:

We peer out, as though through a lens, onto the unfolding events of our lives—a lens fashioned and ground not only by the complexity of our lives but also by the socially supported philosophies, values, and theologies around us, however we take them in. We gradually acquire concepts by which to evaluate our experience, and a vocabulary useful to begin a conversation concerning realities that are essentially beyond our grasp. This becomes our worldview, ever evolving. Loss concentrates our vision, and grieving often requires that we adjust the vocabulary for this dialogue.

It is as though we build a scaffolding out in vast reality, a platform upon which to stand. It is our belief in the stability of that platform that encourages our worldview to grow, serving to calm our terror of being alive yet having to die, of losing, and letting go. The specter of death and the reality of loss challenge the strength of what we have built, affirming the supports of this structure, or demanding overhaul in a major way.[2]

My new worldview reflected a heightened awareness of the significance of both life and death. I became aware of these changes in me as I integrated the death of my father into my ongoing life. At first, I asked the existential questions most survivors ask: *Why did my father suffer? How could God allow this to happen to such a good man? To my family and me? What did we do to deserve this?*

THE FOUR PILLARS OF IDENTITY

These questions challenged my previous assumptions about the world and hopes for what my life would be like. My new worldview incorporated four areas in which I knew I had changed, and I wanted to test them by discovering whether other survivors shared my perceptions. Through my research and inquiry, I found four essential factors that hold the identity together:

1. Our sense of our own mortality
2. Our sense of time flying by, flowing like a stream, or standing still, as well as our relationship with time, as reflected by whether we tend to live in the past, the present, or the future
3. Our values and priorities regarding people and the world around us
4. Our relationship to the world through our connection to family and friends, the community, humankind, or the universe

Concerns regarding these four factors shape the worldview that survivors adopt after their loss and contribute significantly to the new identity and sense of meaning that they develop. In my research, I found that how survivors dealt with issues related to these factors had a critical effect on how they lived their lives and the type of identity and purpose they assumed—consciously and unconsciously.

By raising awareness about your beliefs, worldview, and operating principles, you can develop an identity that is consistent with your perspective. I contend that the way survivors perceive these four factors, and how they are manifested in each identity type, can serve as important predictors of the survivors' well-being and sense of meaning in life.

The Four Pillars and Identity Types

Mortality, orientation toward time, values, and priorities, and relationship to the world we live in: I believe that, after experiencing the death of a loved one, our ideas and perceptions about these complex concepts change. As a result, we form a new identity, a revised sense of self, that contributes to how we see the world and live our lives. Understanding our identity can lead us to our own unique path to healing.

Pillar 1: Our Sense of Our Own Mortality

The first factor I considered was related to how a survivor views the duration of his or her life. Looking back at my life, I now know how the deaths of my father and mother have affected me. Although I was out of touch until recently with how my mother's death had affected my view of my mortality, I was acutely aware of how my father's death had shaped my perspective on life and death. I had drawn intense and immediate lessons about life from his death even though I was only eleven years old at the time. Since my father was thirty-five when he died, I inferred that my life would be short and, therefore, that I must seize every moment in order to make the most of my time on earth.

For many who have lost a loved one, a new sense of mortality emerges. Suddenly, we become aware—if we were not before—of the fact that life is not a permanent condition. We begin to acknowledge our life as finite. Therefore, living—that state of being beyond mere subsistence—assumes a new meaning. Life becomes a precious, limited commodity, a cherished gift to be valued and used wisely. A time-limited view of life tends to cause us to evaluate our priorities. Some may take a "Why bother?" approach, behave recklessly, and view life and death cynically or deny any concerns about mortality. The majority of us, however, acknowledge that "we don't know how long we will live," that life is unpredictable, and that "things happen." We are inspired to set life goals for ourselves while remaining aware that we don't know how long we will be alive to achieve them.

As I evaluated the responses about this issue from those I interviewed, I found that most survivors became more aware of their own mortality. Memorialists, normalizers, and activists tended to share a view of life as finite. As such, many said they wanted to make the most of their life, realizing it is precious. As one activist observed, "I am driven in my work, but I get a lot more done than most people and I feel good about it!"

Based on my analysis of the interviews, I also observed that seekers tended to fear death less than the other identity types, because they perceive themselves in relationship with nonmaterial reality, the part of themselves that they would call their soul. They believe that life is transcendent. Their beliefs ranged from going to heaven to be with God to reincarnation of the soul. On the other end of the identity spectrum, the nomads reflected a cynicism or fatal-ism about life and death: "Ashes to ashes—that's all there is to it." They had lost faith, in God and in themselves. Their grief implied their sense of being victimized: "It's not fair that my wife died." "My father was too young to have a fatal stroke." Although they were unhappy with their lives, they had not yet grasped the significance of their loss suffi-ciently to turn their experience into something from which they could learn and grow.

My conclusion about survivors' awareness of their mortality contributed to understanding what form a new identity would take. I think this awareness should be con-sidered a necessary prerequisite in the process of finding that identity.

Since the death of my parents pervasively affected my sense of my own mortality, I then asked myself: "If we become aware of the fact that we will die at some time in the future, does this knowledge also affect how we will live our lives now?" To answer this question, I focused on three additional factors that I believed could be changed by loss.

PILLAR 2: OUR SENSE OF TIME AND ORIENTATION TOWARD TIME

"Time" is something we are all aware of. For most of us, it represents the way we organize our daily lives—around min-utes, hours, days, and weeks. Time also helps us manage the events of our lives, which occur on a continuum of past, present, and future. With a greater awareness of our mortal-ity, most of us are likely to become even more aware of time in both of these ways.

Although most of us conduct our work and our lives on the basis of time, we may not be aware that the way we live reflects our primary orientation toward time. For example, some of us clearly live in the moment, ignoring the way our experiences have shaped our attitudes or how our behaviors might influence our future. Some, like myself, tend to think ahead, directing their attention toward the future, not always appreciating the present moment. Others live in the past, holding on to memories of the way things were rather than seeing things as they are. I believe that the way we live our lives and the choices we make are significantly influenced by our primary orientation toward time.

Most of the respondents in my research had a primary orientation toward time as "precious." How they lived their lives in relation to their time perspective varied. For example, several parents established scholarship foundations to honor the lives of their teenage children. The primary orientation of these memorialists was toward the past, looking back to their children's lives and preserving their memories. In contrast, a bereaved man in his forties, who admitted thinking about his father "all the time," created a life for his family like the one he had lost at the age of fourteen after his father's death. As a normalizer, he carefully plans a secure and fulfilling "present and future" for his wife and children, because he has learned that "life is unpredictable."

Activists focus on the future. A teacher who turned grief counselor after her ten-year-old daughter's sudden death anticipates the need to create safe places for children and families to share their own grief and adapt to their losses. Her organization's literature notes that "90% of children will be impacted by the death or serious illness of someone close to them by the time they graduate from high school."[3]

Seekers and nomads tend to live in the moment, though the orientation of seekers is rooted in philosophical concepts about life: "All we really know is what is today. We cannot change the past, and we don't know what the future holds." In contrast, a thirty-something nomad whose father died when he was seven may not have found a focus for his life: "Time goes by, and I am just floating along. . . ."

PILLAR 3: OUR VALUES AND PRIORITIES REGARDING PEOPLE AND THE WORLD AROUND US

The third significant factor I pondered is how survivors reevaluate their current lives as a result of their loss. I found considerable evidence in my own research, as well as my broader experience, that innumerable survivors change their priorities, interests, and values about people, society, and the world. I have seen individuals who set aside their original goals for material success, the great job, and the prestigious position; transformed their lives; and redirected their talents toward making a positive impact on the world around them. Often this is demonstrated by taking on a cause related to their loved one's death.

One example is a father whose daughter was killed during the Columbine High School massacre in 1999. He gave up his corporate position and now crusades around the world to prevent youth violence, promoting his daughter's beliefs in compassion and kindness, and her commitment to Jesus's teachings, as his way of improving safety for children and teens.

PILLAR 4: OUR RELATIONSHIP TO THE WORLD

Finally, I wondered how survivors of loss change their perception of the world in which they live. Regardless of where they live, all human beings develop beliefs that tend to validate their existence in a particular reality. This reality represents what I call our "relationship to the world." In this concept, the world is not merely the geographic location of the place where we live; it is a way of life and of understanding our world as each of us experiences it. In its ideal form, the world is rational, orderly, and harmonious. As Janoff-Bulman suggested earlier, we tend to take this understanding for granted. Most adults, as well as children, make assumptions about the world—that it is safe, it is fair and just, and it will always be the same.

In the United States, for example, we have the rights of freedom to express ourselves in ways that contribute to our sense of self. Our lives are relatively predictable from one day to another. Until the September 11 attacks, we felt safe, as individuals and as a country, to pursue our hopes and dreams. In contrast, a war-torn country such as Iraq or Sudan presents its people with a reality that suggests life is dangerous and unpredictable and makes them feel they are at risk of losing their future.

When we experience loss, our relationship to the world often changes. We may no longer feel safe or secure. In the face of such profound insecurity, I found a common thread among those I interviewed: a search for greater connection, meaning, and positive impact on other human beings—whether it was in their families, their work, their community, or at a global level. A noteworthy distinction emerged from the data, however, that also influenced the identity these individuals adopted. I noted two distinct patterns of response, consisting of what I term "inward" and "outward" worldviews.

Inward worldview. The survivors with an inward worldview tended to focus on the self, the family, and the community in which they live. The priorities of greatest concern were the well-being of those closest to them. Their interests and concerns were directed toward immediate and close-at-hand issues and needs. They tended to view the world as a place that holds memories of sad times or experiences as well as potential disappointments. Their energy was directed toward counteracting the negative experiences of the past with positive ones in the present and future. They chose to shape lives in which they could feel they have some control.

Outward worldview. In contrast, the other group of respondents seemed to be more focused on people, the world, and life as it relates to the "family of man" and the universe. Their primary focus tended to be on exploring universal and far-reaching issues. As a result of their loss experience, they concluded that they had been placed on earth for a specific purpose—to help others, to create, to make an impact on the quality of life, in whatever ways seemed appropriate. Their interests and priorities tended to involve the social and global needs of the world; thus, they typically exhibited an outward worldview. Their perspective more often recognized the connectedness of all things and perceived the relationships between humans and other natural systems.

CREATING MEANING FROM OUR LOSS

In the Old Testament, the Book of Job asks us why God allows good people to suffer. Satan had challenged God to test the faith of one of his devoted servants, Job. To win the bet, God destroyed Job's home and cattle, killed his children, and inflicted painful boils on his body. Job raised his hands and cried to the heavens, questioning God's justice: "He has torn me in his wrath, and hated me!"[4] Why had God caused him, a good man, such misery?

From the writing of this story almost three thousand years ago to the current time, we humans have asked "Why?" in response to a multitude of injustices inflicted upon people throughout the world. Events such as wars, natural disasters, terrorist attacks, and terminal illnesses all result in momentous losses of human life and leave pain and suffering in their wake.

Neimeyer believes that "meaning reconstruction in response to loss is the central process in grieving."[5] As human beings, it is our nature to make meaning and create significance in matters that affect our lives. It is the manifestation of both our intellectual capacity and our spiritual disposition, our ability to look inward and outward simultaneously. He suggests that when we lose a loved one, our life is disrupted. As human beings, we require order in our lives and create expectations for relationships, events, and dreams. He observes that our ability to make sense of a death and to find some benefits from the loss experience is a meaning-making process. Accomplishing this task is critical to the successful reconstruction of a survivor's identity and long-term recovery from loss.[6]

The experience of loss confronts us with a search for meaning. First, it is the quest for answers, explanations for why our loved ones died. Why did they suffer? Why has losing them caused us to suffer as well? Intellectually, we want to know that everything that could have been done—to save them, treat them, make them comfortable—was done. When people die of a terminal illness, and we have been with them, participated in the experience with them, and cared for them, we may have the opportunity to learn these answers—through our conversations and observations as well as through such caregivers as physicians, therapists, and clergy.

When the death is sudden, however, caused by an accident, a violent act, or a disaster, or when the one we loved committed suicide, dropped dead without warning, or was a child of any age who preceded his or her parents in death, rational explanations are harder to come by. We often rely for answers on spiritual avenues—religious or existential understandings: *God had a plan. All life is suffering. We will find meaning from the suffering.*

But these explanations, whatever they may be, can work only if they are consistent with one's worldview and beliefs. For example, some survivors, like Job, might remain faithful to their beliefs, their traditions, and their God. Others might reject the God who could have caused such suffering and shattered their lives. Finding acceptable answers through either means can be difficult. As Rabbi Harold Kushner says, "Sometimes there is no reason. What is important is to focus not on why the tragedy happened, but where it will lead you. We must focus on the world's goodness."[7] Drawing on the work of Dorothee Soelle, a German theologian, he suggests that meaning can be found through exploration of ourselves:

> If suffering and death in someone close to us brings us to explore the limits of our capacity for strength and love and cheerfulness, if it leads us to discover sources of consolation we never knew before, then *we* make the person a witness for the affirmation of life rather than its rejection.[8]

Another scholar, Pesach Krauss, builds on this definition of meaning as "achieved only when we relate to other human beings or to a cause greater than ourselves."[9]

The quest for meaning leads us to what I consider the following fundamental questions related to loss:

1. What have I learned about myself and the world around me?

2. What is truly important to me?
3. How can I create a life that is fulfilling, rewarding, and impactful?
4. What is the purpose of my life?
5. Who do I want to be as a result of my loss experience?

Finding meaning and purpose in life is the basis for creating our new identity. This task is essential both for resolving our losses and for our healing. Each of us must figure it out for ourselves.

OUR IDENTITY AND HOW IT CHANGES FROM LOSS

Identity is who we are—in relation to our world of family, friends, and community. It is how we represent our "self" to our social world. It is our unique composite of experience, values, knowledge, and all that life exposes us to. Since our identity is often linked to someone we love, death requires survivors to define a new sense of self, and even *reality*, without their loved one. Identity, as psychoanalyst Erik Erikson proposed, is also a requisite for intimate relationships.[10] Bereavement experts deem "assuming a new identity" to be one of the most important tasks of grieving. New identity formation is therefore critical to adjusting to loss, returning to healthy functioning, and developing new relationships, including intimate ones.

Erikson first coined the term *identity crisis* to describe the most important conflict human beings encounter when they go through what he proposed as the eight developmental stages in life.[11] Although Erikson theorized that this crisis first appears as children reach their teens, subsequent thinkers have suggested that we can experience crises throughout our lives. Author Gail Sheehy popularized this idea in her best-selling book, *Passages*, illustrating the significant transitions that we confront as we go through life.[12] Clearly, when we lose a loved one, we are plunged into a state of crisis.

Sociologists tell us that we define ourselves—as a mother, father, spouse, daughter, brother, child with two parents—as one way of organizing our world. We assume certain roles and create a piece of our "self" in relation to others. Our beliefs, our values, and our direction in life are often shaped by those we love. Clea Simon, writing in *Fatherless Women*, describes how fathers often influence their daughters by infusing such confidence in them that the daughters can see that all things are possible.[13]

When we lose that person, however, we also lose a sense of who we are. For example, one woman shared with me this description of the aftermath of her son's death in a car accident:

> I had trouble focusing on my work for months. I didn't know who I was anymore. Was I still his mother? Would people see me as a mother? And what about my daughter? Would she still be a sister if her brother was dead? Those around us often didn't understand this. They expected us to return to our old selves, but we couldn't. We didn't know who we were.

Dr. Therese Rando, a leading clinical psychologist, researcher, and international consultant who writes prolifically about the many aspects of grief, explains:

> Your identity changes as you slowly make the change from a "we" to an "I." This is caused by the necessity of responding to the new world without the deceased, which

demands that you take on new ways of being, thinking, and feeling in the world to reflect the reality that he is dead. You will have to give up or modify certain hopes, expectations, and experiences you had with your loved one, and you must develop new ones. . . . You must adopt new roles, skills, behaviors, and relationships.[14]

Confronting the reality of having to live a changed life requires that you accept that your view of the world will change. Your loved one is gone physically. Psychologically, your sense of identity, security, and safety are gone. Socially, relationships with family and friends may change. Spiritually, you may feel abandoned by God and isolated from others. Not knowing who you are or where to go next, you are now faced with the most challenging task of all—creating a new identity and starting over in the business of living.

As noted in the introduction, thanatologist and philosopher Thomas Attig calls this challenge "relearning the world."[15] It involves adapting to a changed physical and social world and redefining our relationship to the person we lost. Most important, we are compelled to ask ourselves: Who am I? What choices do I have? How can I create meaning from my loss? Who will I be in my new life? Since developing a new identity is an important task in the grieving process, finding that new self, that new identity, challenges us to find the answers to these critical questions. For most of us, this is a daunting task.

GRIEF AS A DOORWAY TO HOPE

Although I have been an orphan for more than half my life, only in the past five years have I reached another level of understanding about how the deaths of my parents affected me. This revelation has given me some sense of peace. And, while most people would assume I have "gotten over" my losses, I know that if being bereaved is being deprived of our loved ones, I remain in a state of bereavement. I still remember the dates of my parents' deaths, birthdays, and wedding anniversary as vividly as I do my daughter's birthday. On those days, I still feel a twinge of sadness about how their absence deprived me of role models for managing my life, support during hard times, and the joys of sharing the happiness of our mutual achievements.

My journey of understanding, like that of the Jews in the desert, has taken forty years. I now understand what a far-ranging impact the deaths of my father and, seventeen years later, my mother have had on me and my family. I have spent much of my life asking questions about why this happened, what effect their deaths had on me and my family, and what contributions I could make to those who have had similar experiences. I have learned lessons about life and death, and these lessons have guided me—for better and worse—throughout my life. They have changed the way I see myself, the world, and my place in it. I am certain that the deaths of my father and mother served as catalysts that guided me toward a particular path in my life, influenced who I have become, the choices I have made, and the ways I have lived my life. As a result, I believe I am a wiser, more life-affirming, and more courageous human being than I might otherwise have been.

In her book *Prodigal Summer*, best-selling author Barbara Kingsolver tells the story of a young scientist, Lusa, who, after being suddenly widowed, successfully manages the family farm, earning the respect of her previously critical sisters-in-law. In explaining how her husband's death affected her, she offers insight into how survivors can be transformed:

I was mad at him for dying and leaving me here, at first. Pissed off like you wouldn't believe. But now I'm starting to think he wasn't supposed to be my whole life, he was just this *doorway* to me. I am so grateful to him for that.[16]

Two

The Nomad

Do you know where you're going to?
Do you like the things that life is showing you?
Where are you going to?
Do you know?
      —Theme from *Mahogany*, M. Masser and G. Goffin

IN THE DAYS, WEEKS, AND MONTHS immediately after a significant loss, we are all nomads. We experience a sense of unreality that this unimaginable event has occurred. We suffer a range of emotions, thoughts, and physical sensations. We operate on automatic pilot to cope with our pervasive confusion and shock. We don't know who we are or what we should be doing.

In her memoir *The Year of Magical Thinking*, esteemed author Joan Didion writes about her initial reaction to the sudden death of her husband, fellow writer, and soul mate John Gregory Dunne, who died of a massive heart attack while she was in the kitchen preparing dinner. "There was a level on which I believed that what had happened remained reversible. . . . I needed to be alone so that he could come back."[1]

Symptoms of Acute Grieving

- *Feelings:* sadness, anger, anxiety, loneliness, fatigue, helplessness, shock, numbness, yearning, emancipation, relief
- *Physical sensations:* weakness, lethargy, breathlessness, tightness in chest or stomach
- *Cognitions:* disbelief, confusion, preoccupation, hallucinations, dreams, magical thinking
- *Behaviors:* sleep disturbances, appetite changes, social withdrawal, absentmindedness, restlessness, crying

Nomads seem to sleepwalk through their daily lives. They tend to live in the moment, clouded by sad memories, lacking clarity about their values and life priorities, unsure of their faith in God, and unfocused about the meaning of their life and how they fit in the world. Putting one foot in front of the other, they may go to work, spend more time with family, have dinner with friends, to seek comfort and escape from the loneliness and emptiness their loved one used to fill. This behavior is a normal response to loss, particularly sudden and unexpected loss.

Nomads are typically "lost in transition." William Bridges, a writer and consultant on life transitions, has written extensively on this topic, including his own career and personal transitions. His books have helped countless others to make sense of transitions due to personal losses, such as divorce and death, and workplace changes, such as layoffs, retirement, or career change. In *The Way of Transition: Embracing Life's Most Difficult Moments,* he writes poignantly of his wife Mondi's death and his own trying shifts of identity from husband to widower. He asserts that the "meandering pathway across the void"[2] was necessary to continue his life.

Bridges explains that every transition involves an ending, followed by a period of confusion and distress that leads to a new beginning. Nomads have experienced the ending. Their loved one has died. After the anguish of acknowledging this, they move into what Bridges refers to as the "neutral zone." It is the empty space between the old life and the new.[3] Within this void, however, much work must be accomplished in order to move through this transition successfully. It is the labor of inner change, a personal journey involving ups and downs, highs and lows—not the sort, Bridges warns us, that one can consciously set out to accomplish. This "space" is where the grieving must occur, where a new identity and an adjustment to life without that person begins to form.

LOSS AND THE GRIEVING PROCESS

Grieving is the complex journey we must make to understand what has happened to our lives and adjust to the many changes the loss has brought us. Grief is a normal emotional reaction of all bereaved human beings. The process of grieving occurs over time and allows us to adapt to our loss and accept the reality that our loved one is gone. Like infants and young children who feel distress at being separated from their mothers, adults experience the pain of being separated from a loved one. They also feel a sense of vulnerability about what their life will be like as they face it alone.

By the end of this process, the majority of those who have lost a loved one have worked through their grief, found ways of staying connected to their loved one, adapted to their changed life, and resumed some sense of normalcy—though, of course, their lives are never quite the same again. They have made the transition from speaking about the person who "is" to speaking about the person who "was." They have found a new identity without their loved one. They have successfully completed their journey through the neutral zone and shed their nomad status.

ESSENCE OF THE NOMAD IDENTITY TYPE

A well-known example of the nomad identity type is shown in the Oscar-nominated film *You Can Count on Me*, written and directed by Kenneth Lonergan, which tells the story of a sister and a brother, Sammy and Terry Prescott, whose parents are killed suddenly in a horrific car accident one dark night. Flash forward, twenty years later, when Sammy is a single mother, living in a small upstate New York town, in the same house in which she grew up, with her adorable eight-year-old son, Rudy. She works at a bank, goes to church on Sundays, and lives a safe, albeit dull, life in the comfort and security of her hometown. In contrast, her brother, Terry, has been wandering from state to state, working odd jobs, occasionally doing time in jail, when she receives his letter saying that he plans to visit. Charming, irresponsible, and extremely self-destructive, Terry decides to stay around, to the delight of his sister and her son. Rudy initially bonds with his uncle, who becomes a "father figure," but Terry proves unreliable and soon deeply hurts Rudy. In frustration, Sammy ultimately asks her brother to leave.

Lonergan's film offers an excellent example of how loss impacts survivor identity. While Sammy and Terry have remained close over the intervening years, they clearly made divergent choices for their lives. When Terry reveals that he's gotten his girlfriend in trouble, Sammy ruefully exclaims that she wishes "Mom was here." "No one knows what to do with you," she goes on. He answers: "I know how they feel." When Sammy asks him if he goes to church anymore, Terry's loss of faith, a symptom of the nomad identity, becomes apparent:

> Terry: No, because it's ridiculous . . . primitive . . . a fairy tale.

> Sammy: Has it ever occurred to you that that's what's making it so difficult for you? You've lost hold of any kind of anchor, not just your religious feelings. Any kind of trust in anything. No wonder you drift around so much. How would you know if you found the right thing?

> Terry: I'm not looking for anything; I just want to "get on with it"![4]

When Sammy and Terry lost their parents, they lost the relationships they had enjoyed with them, the experiences they shared, and their status as members of an intact family. Parents act as teachers, role models, and advisers. They provide not just the necessities of life but also a sense of safety and security. They teach us values and how to behave. When children are confused or frightened, parents provide support and guidance about how to live in the world. When Sammy and Terry lost their parents, they lost their way of life as they had known it. Consciously or not, Sammy and Terry changed their view of the world from the moment they learned of their parents' deaths. That loss transformed their sense of themselves and the way their lives would move forward. Each responded uniquely to their new situation, acquiring a post-loss identity. Sammy was able to find herself by staying in their home and community, but Terry was not.

Although Sammy chose a path as a normalizer (an identity type discussed in chapter 4), it is clear that Terry is still a nomad twenty years later. He literally wanders from state to state. He does not know where he belongs in the world. He is an "emotional drifter," who smokes dope and cigarettes, drinks beer, and zones out in front of the TV. These habits are ways of avoiding the pain of mourning his parents, even twenty years after their death. His sadness is palpable; all of his choices reflect his sense of futility. Terry's visit with his sister and nephew ultimately fails—not because Sammy asks him to leave but because Terry refuses to confront his pent-up feelings of grief, anger, and confusion when she challenges him to examine his current path.

COMPLICATED GRIEF
When Acute Grief Leads to a Long-Term Nomad

What happens to the estimated 15 percent of bereaved[5] like Terry who don't make it through the normal grieving process? Their behavior presents risks of what grief experts call "complicated grief." Sudden and untimely deaths, such as the auto crash that killed Terry and Sammy's parents, can heighten the impact of any loss. Heart attacks, strokes, suicides, or deaths by violent means are also included in this category. Because these deaths are unanticipated, they can leave the survivors in a state of shock and disbelief longer than the deaths for which we can prepare, such as those caused by a terminal illness.

"Ambiguous loss"—when a loved one is never found and survivors are not sure if their loved one is living or dead—may also lead to complicated grief. Dr. Pauline Boss, professor of family social science at the University of Minnesota, coined this phrase to describe situations in which survivors must live with uncertainty for months, years, perhaps even a lifetime.[6] Think of the thousands of wives and children of soldiers who never returned from their wartime service. I occasionally spot bumper stickers reminding us to remember MIAs (those who are missing in action) from the Vietnam War. Other examples include the millions of families torn apart as they were taken to the Nazi concentration camps, the eleven thousand people called "the disappeared" from Argentina who were victims of a brutal dictatorship, and the four thousand children who were missing or displaced after Hurricane Katrina. In situations such as these, survivors face a greater likelihood of having "unfinished business."

When the grieving process does not follow the predictable patterns of working through emotions—acknowledging the loss, resolving unfinished business with the deceased, and adjusting to and accepting a new life—it is considered "complicated mourning." The symptoms of complicated mourning include an inability to enjoy life or accomplish ordinary tasks, a deep and prolonged depression, and a sense of not knowing who you are or what your life is about. If you cannot deal with the reality of your loss after it occurs, or if you deny that it has had an effect on you, your grieving process may be prolonged for months or even years.

I call these survivors nomads because they remain stuck in their grieving process for a variety of reasons. First, they may deny that the loss affected them, as Terry did, and avoid the painful yet necessary feelings that would allow them to accept their loss. Second, they may resist letting go of their loved one, pretending that he or she will come back, as Didion did. Or they may believe that they are different, their relationship was unique, and no one can possibly understand their grief. Third, they may have conflicting feelings about the person who died. For example, one woman I spoke with had been very angry with her husband before he died in a car crash. Similarly, some survivors of September 11 victims admitted having had a petty argument with their loved one that morning, which left them with an intense sense of guilt in the aftermath.

Symptoms That Are Likely to Indicate "Complicated Grief"[7]

- Intrusive thoughts, yearning, searching for the deceased, excessive loneliness since the death
- Subjective sense of numbness, detachment, or absence of emotional responsiveness
- Difficulty acknowledging the death (disbelief)
- Sense of purposelessness or feelings of futility about the future
- Feeling that life is empty or meaningless
- Feeling that part of oneself has died
- Shattered worldview
- Assumption that symptoms or harmful behaviors are related to the deceased
- Excessive irritability, bitterness, or anger related to the death
- Clinically significant impairment in social, occupational, or other important areas of functioning
- Continuation of symptoms for at least six months

Unresolved Grief

Unresolved feelings such as these challenge normal recovery from grief. Several of the people who told me their stories of unresolved grief were a woman whose younger brother was killed in the North Tower of the World Trade Center on September 11, 2001; a woman in her midthirties from Ireland who harbored intense anger toward her mother almost twenty years after her father's fatal heart attack; and a fifty-plus man whose father had died when he was seven years old and who claimed that he had lost his role model for manhood. Years or even decades later, these individuals remained nomads, still struggling with unresolved grief that emotionally crippled them and prevented them from enjoying a fulfilling life.

I found that unresolved grief is the common thread that binds nomads together. They have been unable or unwilling to face their grief and go through all the complex yet necessary steps of the grieving process. But their avoidance, conscious or unconscious, has only postponed the inevitable work of grieving. As a result, long after their loss, these nomads lacked a clear sense of who they were and what their life was about.

PROFILES OF NOMADS

The following stories of real-life nomads highlight the major characteristics of each person's loss experience and exemplify the themes and patterns of the nomad identity.

Cheryl: A Story of Traumatic Loss

The survivors of the September 11 terrorist attacks experienced sudden, violent losses that brought a multitude of uncertainties. Thousands of family members lost loved ones at the World Trade Center, at the Pentagon, and aboard the four hijacked planes. More than ten thousand children lost one or even both parents in the Twin Towers alone; many wives lost young husbands; parents mourned adult children. There are innumerable media stories about the impact of these deaths on the survivors' lives. Cheryl lost her adored younger brother Allan.

As we sat at Cheryl's kitchen table more than two years after the attacks, she told me her story about losing Allan, and the memories of that day poured out of her. Allan was twenty-three years younger than Cheryl, born during her father's second marriage, and Cheryl regarded him more like a son than a younger brother. Cheryl said Allan didn't work in the World Trade Center and had gone there only to represent his company at a meeting being held at the Windows on the World restaurant atop the North Tower. He was running late that morning and arrived at the building just before the first plane hit. Cheryl said wistfully, "If only he had been a few minutes later. . . ."

Allan had been married only one year before, and at the insistence of his wife, Judy, they had become pregnant almost immediately. On September 11, they were anticipating the imminent birth of their first child. Their son, Adam, was born six days later, on September 17, 2001. Although Cheryl credits Judy with maintaining family ties with Allan's parents and siblings, she struggles with what the relationship will be in the future, as her attractive young sister-in-law inevitably moves on with her life. Cheryl described herself as feeling "so sad" and being unable to get up and go to work, saying, "It's like I have lead in my feet." She also found herself increasingly worried about her own children. "People say I should go on with my life," Cheryl said, "but I don't know how to do that."

The effects of the suddenness of Allan's death, the violence that caused it, and the uncertainty about her future relationship with his son all contribute to Cheryl's sadness and sense of confusion.

DISENFRANCHISED GRIEF

Added to these issues, Cheryl had not found answers to many key questions that might allow her to resolve her sense of helplessness about the event and Allan's ill-fated presence at the World Trade Center that day. How did Allan's company honor his memory? What happened to the femur bone unearthed in the disaster's rubble that was identified as Allan's many months later?

As Cheryl searched for answers to her questions, another painful reality struck her. As the *sister* of the victim, Cheryl discovered that she did not have the same rights to information as her brother's wife. After Allan's death, Judy was the acknowledged point of contact with city representatives regarding identification, settlement issues, and the media. Even when a femur bone was found to match Cheryl's DNA, Judy, not Cheryl, was contacted. As close as Cheryl had been to Allan, she was, from an official standpoint, *only* his sister. While the media pursued her sister-in-law and nephew, who appeared on prime-time talk shows such as *Good Morning America* and in *People* magazine, Cheryl felt that *her* loss, as a sister, went largely unrecognized.

Dr. Kenneth Doka, a pioneer in the field of bereavement, characterized this phenomenon as "disenfranchised grief," when social norms perceive certain relationships and losses to be less significant. For example, bereaved who have lost lovers, close friends, colleagues, nieces and nephews, and siblings are often neglected, unacknowledged, or avoided. Other people frequently fail to recognize their right to grieve or validate the pain they experienced. Referring to the September 11 terrorist attacks, Doka predicted:

> Despite high levels of support and immediate intervention, there are likely to be many persons whose grief will be disenfranchised . . . including police and firefighters, who lost colleagues, as well as others within and outside the World Trade Center, the hijacked planes, the Pentagon, and the field in Pennsylvania who experienced the deaths of friends, neighbors, coworkers, and even adult children and siblings.[8]

Cheryl's experience provided numerous examples of this phenomenon of disenfranchised grief. She recounted an incident in her office at a well-respected university on the morning of the attacks. As she gradually learned of Allan's presence in the North Tower, several associates made caring gestures of support, but others reacted with what Cheryl called "unbelievable insensitivity," trading stories of pleasurable visits to New York in the period before the attacks.

During the weeks and months that followed, she was further disappointed by the lack of support from close friends. No one brought her food, a common and traditional way of offering comfort to the bereaved during the mourning period. Few called to check on how Cheryl was doing. Acknowledging that she was viewed as an independent, competent career woman who didn't need anyone to "take care of her," she smiled gloomily and observed that during the past two years, she had gained lots of weight, eating nothing more than Kit Kats every night because she lacked the energy to cook a meal. The coup de grâce was a close friend's chastising Cheryl for neglecting *her* and flippantly remarking, "Well, Allan's death was two years ago." This insensitive comment was a clear example of how limited many people in our society are in understanding both the pain of the grieving process and the lifelong impact of loss on survivors, particularly if others perceive them to have had less significant relationships with the deceased.

Loss of a Sibling

The siblings of the deceased suffer not only a sense of loss but also a sense of their place in the family. Their role in relation to their parents and one another changes. Their brother or sister was sometimes a companion in family activities, sometimes a competitor for their parents' attention. Depending on the ages of the surviving children, they may suffer an irrational sense of guilt—that they survived, that they might have been in some way responsible for their sibling's death, or that they could have prevented it. Siblings often suffer this "survivor guilt," wishing it had been *they* who died. They may develop false beliefs that they were somehow responsible and that they deserve punishment.

In other cases, surviving siblings may believe that they are less worthy of being loved and appreciated for who they are. These feelings of inadequacy can be increased when parents become emotionally absent from their surviving children as they struggle to cope with their own grief.

In Judith Guest's poignant 1976 novel *Ordinary People,*[9] Conrad, the younger of two brothers, has attempted suicide due to the guilt he feels at having survived a sailing accident in which his older and much-adored brother, Buck, died. Conrad and his parents exhibit strongly contrasting styles of grieving. Conrad is not only tormented by a sense of failure for letting his brother drown but also senses that Buck was his mother's favorite and believes his mother now hates him.

Conrad's mother denies her own grief and tries to get the family's life back to "normal," as we shall see in chapter 4 ("The Normalizer"). His father, in contrast, demonstrates real concern by encouraging Conrad to see a psychiatrist after he is released from the hospital following his suicide attempt. Though initially reluctant, Conrad does follow up and forms a trusting relationship with the highly skilled Dr. Berger, who helps him unravel his memory of the traumatic event: it was Buck's letting go of the boat that caused him to drown. As a result, Conrad is able to confront the reality of his brother's death, grieve him openly and honestly, and begin his healing process.

In order to restore healthy individual and family functioning, it is essential to understand the dynamics in the family, the relationships of the siblings with one another and with their parents before the death, and the multifaceted impact of the death on the surviving siblings.

Physical and Symbolic Losses

In addition to the physical loss of her brother Allan, Cheryl experienced the *symbolic* loss of her self-perceived status as "grandmother" to Allan's son, Adam. Symbolic losses are intangible losses that relate to the psychosocial aspect of the relationship. Since she was so much older than her brother, Cheryl felt more like Allan's mother than his sister, a feeling that influenced her sense of herself and her identity. As a consequence of the loss, her status as "big sister" resulted in an almost immediate shift in family roles for her and her parents in relation to Allan's wife, Judy, and their son, Adam. Judy understandably preferred to grieve with her parents. After all, she had been married only a year and had not yet developed close ties with Allan's family. Now Cheryl wondered how they would communicate and whether they would continue to share family gatherings with Allan's son for holidays and birthdays.

How has Allan's death affected Cheryl? She says that she is a changed person. She is more concerned about the safety of her daughters, more aware of everyone's mortality and the value of every day. As her sister-in-law moves on with a new family, Cheryl is struggling with what kind of relationship she and her family can expect to have with her nephew Adam. How can she find meaning and purpose from her unbearable loss? What will her new identity be?

MOVING TOWARD RESOLUTION

If Cheryl is to heal from her loss, she must find answers to these questions. She must create an identity that clarifies her relationship to her brother's wife and son. She must find meaning from the senseless death of her beloved brother. She must discover how she can honor Allan's life and his death so that she can remain connected to him and his young family. If Cheryl fails to resolve her grief, she runs the risk of remaining a nomad, periodically suffering painful triggers that remind her of Allan and his son and invoke images of an anticipated future that can never come to pass.

The losses of September 11 were intensely public. As Cheryl's story illustrates, finding a new identity when reminders of the tragedy remain in the public consciousness may prolong the grieving process, impede healing, and make some survivors more vulnerable to developing complications. As a result, we need to be aware of the risk factors for nomads.

Denial Triggered by Grief

More subtle and private losses, however, can also take their toll. For instance, in families that experience alcoholism and other addictions, family members tend to keep silent, harboring feelings of shame and guilt, and colluding in cover-ups to protect them from the disapproval of the community. But that silence cannot prevent the personal pain that develops from a lack of openness and honesty. As psychologist Dr. Claudia Black, a well-known expert on alcoholism and its lifelong impact, explains:

> Denial is a defense mechanism, a natural response to protect against pain. When someone feels helpless to impact their situation or is ashamed of what is occurring, they often resort to denial. Denial can be identified when individuals discount, minimize, or rationalize their feelings. . . . While the word *denial* is most often associated with the addictive family, it is the central dynamic of any dysfunctional family.[10]

We are all brought up to believe that "family" is the place where we feel secure, protected, and accepted for who we are. When a family does not provide its members with this sense of safety, they can feel lost, alone, and emotionally abandoned. The following story illustrates how one woman's family secret was compounded by the death of a parent and sibling, leading to confusion, fear, and her protracted struggle for identity.

Deidre: The Burden of Multiple Losses

When I first met Deidre, an attractive thirty-six-year-old blonde who had immigrated to the United States from

Ireland eight years before, we were at a personal growth workshop at which participants were sharing life stories and trying to address unresolved issues. Stepping up to the microphone to speak to the group, Deidre explained that she had a difficult time making decisions about her future. She was very angry with her mother, who was still living in Ireland with her five siblings and their families. "Why?" the leader asked her. Deidre confessed that she blamed her mother for causing her father's death seventeen years earlier.

One day, while driving Deidre and her younger brother David to work in downtown Dublin, her father had collapsed behind the wheel. After being transported via ambulance to a hospital, he was pronounced dead of a heart attack. She recalled that in the period leading up to the attack, her father had lost weight. He had also suffered an angina attack three weeks earlier and had taken time off from work, which Deidre said was "unusual" for him. He had resorted to hot milk with pepper, which Deidre called "an old wives' remedy," in order to "sweat it out of him," not realizing that his condition was life-threatening. She even remembered that he'd drunk only half his tea before getting in the car that fatal day. "Afterward," she observed, "you think about what more you could've done and what you would do differently." In retrospect, Deidre felt tremendous guilt. Since her mother was an alcoholic, Deidre had often performed the role of making her father's dinner and fixing his tea. She "adored" him, wanted his approval, and got it. "I knew he loved me," she told me, "but I was busy with my own life, school, friends, work, parties, as teenagers are, and I guess I didn't notice how sick he was." Here's how Deidre described her reaction in the period immediately following her father's death:

His death stopped me in my tracks. I was numb for a long, long time. Though people think a year has passed and you should be OK, I was still trying to fathom it. I started drinking; I was very much in a daze, wasn't fun to be around, canceled plans with friends. I was trying to fill the void and feel OK.

Then, Deidre said, "because big, strong daddies are not supposed to die," she "made up a story in [her] own mind," fantasizing that her father "was down in the country, and that when the funeral was over, he would call [her] brothers and sisters about getting a house, [they would] live together down there, and [they] would be fine." Deidre told me that she was nineteen at the time and that the fantasy continued for the next seventeen years.

When a loved one dies, we may rely on many coping mechanisms—healthy and unhealthy—to help us go on living. Some people self-medicate with alcohol and other drugs to deaden their emotional pain. Others, commonly young children, turn to "magical thinking" in order to deny the reality of the loss and feel more control.

Since her mother was an alcoholic, Deidre may have been predisposed to drink excessively when she was feeling so vulnerable. Although Deidre was older than most children who develop fantasies of their loved one's returning after death, her dependency on her father may have exacerbated her need to hold on to him in this way. Her father's death merely compounded the family's problems.

Four years later, at twenty-three, Deidre was still aimless. Looking for a purpose, she decided to leave her family and go on an adventure by obtaining a position as an au pair in New Jersey. Once she got to the United States, however, she found the responsibility of long days taking care of the children (whom she loved) isolating and burdensome. Her drinking escalated.

GRIEF OVERLOAD

Eight months after she took the au pair position, Deidre was hit with another jolt. She learned that her dearly loved younger brother Daniel had accidentally drowned. Returning home to Ireland, she assumed family responsibilities and tried to comfort her mother, sisters, and one remaining brother. Daniel's sudden death reminded them of the pain and emptiness they had felt from her father's death four years before. This second loss exacerbated Deidre's grief and that of her family. Without grieving her brother's death, or engaging her mother and siblings in examining its effects on the family, Deidre, a natural caregiver, continued going through the motions of caring for her family. Five years passed.

When she decided to return to the United States, Deidre was still drinking and floating along. "The years just added up," she told me, while she remained in limbo, tormented by her inability to make decisions about where she belonged: "Should I go back, but do I want to? Should I stay here and buy a condo? Settle down? I won't even commit to car payments!"

Deidre's behavior illustrates problems nomads often exhibit. First, she did not accept the reality of her father's death. Her magical thinking had kept him alive for many years. Second, mainly through her drinking, Deidre had not allowed herself to experience the pain of losing him, which is something she needed to do. When a loved one leaves them, people can feel many emotions besides sadness. Deidre needed to explore not just the anger she felt toward her mother for what Deidre perceived to be her role in her father's death but also the anger she felt toward her *father* for leaving her. Finally, her inability to make commitments in her life reflected Deidre's deep distrust of the world. If her father could die, and then Daniel, other bad things could happen, too. Better not to invest in anyone or anything for fear of losing it.

Moving toward Resolution

Deidre's attendance at the personal growth workshop where I met her was a positive step in confronting her deeply held feelings. She let the facilitator guide her through an emotional yet cathartic process of working through the pain of her grief. She did not find complete resolution during that workshop experience, but she was well on her way. Next, she would have to adjust to the world in which she acknowledged the deaths of her father and brother, and free herself of her pain and anger, so that she could pursue an empathetic relationship with her mother, revive a closeness with her surviving siblings, and discover who she was and what she now wanted in life.

Children's Understanding of Grief

Young children do not understand the abstract concept of death, so they tend to make up stories to pretend that their lost loved one has gone away and will return. Over time, they come to accept that the deceased will not return, and they can let go. With children under the age of thirteen, the relationship to the parent usually involves an intense attachment. Unless maternal-child bonding does not occur (and sometimes it doesn't), most young children who lose a parent are likely to have vulnerabilities related to their real dependency needs for both survival and emotional support. This was true for Terry, who was about eight years old when his parents were killed in the car crash. For Deidre, the dependency on her father was related to the tight bond they had formed in response to her alcoholic—and emotionally absent—mother.

Teenagers are cognitively capable of grasping the concept of death as final and universal. They regard themselves as immortal and invincible until confronted with the death of a friend, a peer, a parent, or someone else close to them. Unlike younger children, they become much more in touch with their own vulnerability, mortality, and the dangers of living in the world. Given their developmental struggle with finding their identity, the loss of a loved one may either accelerate their growth or set them back into bouts of depression, anger, or rage, which can have an adverse impact.

Parents and other adults must pay attention to the behaviors of children and teens experiencing loss. We can respond as role models by showing our own grief and supporting our children's grief by finding appropriate resources to help them deal with it. Many schools have counselors who help their students with grief and other kinds of losses. Community organizations, such as Centers for Grieving Children, are becoming more prevalent, offering outlets for children's emotions. Consulting with a specialist about any concerns is always a viable option. Finally, after a child or teen suffers a loss, we must observe changes in behavior at home, at school, and with friends and take quick action to resolve any problems.

Steve: A Reappearance of Grief

Many of my interviewees shared with me the anxiety they experienced when reminded of a loss at different points in their lives. The pain of such losses can be triggered by a trivial TV commercial, a sentimental novel, a significant public event such as September 11, or a conversation overheard at the supermarket. Steve, a successful fortyish man I interviewed who had lost his mother when he was in his teens, described his reaction to watching the Golden Globe Awards on television recently. When a TV producer around Steve's age rushed to the podium to accept an award, he launched into the obligatory acknowledgments, first mentioning the actors and other professionals who had contributed to his success. He then thanked his parents, both for their belief in his talent and for their ongoing emotional and financial support during his rise to the top. In Steve's words: "My heart flinched. What a gift to have such unequivocal parental love! I was reminded that I had not had this kind of love and support for more than half of my lifetime. I felt so sad."

How Grief Can Reverberate throughout Our Lives

Individuals such as Steve who lost someone they love in childhood but subsequently developed a strong identity and self-esteem and may otherwise lead happy, successful lives as adults can sometimes revert to behaving like nomads. They may find their current identity challenged many years after their loss, when events such as marrying, having a baby, recalling an anniversary, reaching the same age as the parent at the time of his or her death, or even watching an innocuous TV show may trigger painful feelings that cause survivors to "regrieve" their loss or resume an unfinished grieving process. In more extreme cases, unresolved issues can pop up later in life when sparked by a more direct association with the loss or by a public trauma.

Author William Styron, writing in *Darkness Visible: A Memoir of Madness,* claimed that problems that plagued him as an adult, including alcoholism and depression, were related to the death of his mother when he was thirteen. "Some of my problems I think came from a continuing anguish over my mother's death."[11] Styron's intense bouts of depression as an adult reflected the unresolved grief he must have experienced as an adolescent whose sense of invincibility and dreams for the future were shattered.

Steve's story and other stories throughout this book illustrate that people who lose loved ones in childhood are more likely to become nomads in adulthood, due to their natural vulnerability and lack of a fully developed self at the time of their loss. Their problems are best addressed when they appear. Just as an injured elbow or a broken ankle can heal and function normally again, a broken heart is resilient. The wounds from the loss of a loved one create enduring scars that can periodically itch or throb or ache, and remind us throughout our lives that we will always miss certain experiences we didn't have and must work through these issues again.

APPARENT ADVANTAGES OF BEING A NOMAD

Some might see the nomad as a pragmatic person such as Terry, who "gets on with life," doing what needs to be done to survive. He avoids introspection and mourning and tells himself that loss is a part of life. Others might regard a nomad as being like Cheryl, very strong, steady, and apparently able to cope well, even while suffering intense grief. From this perspective, the nomad may be viewed as a true survivor, valued highly in our "rugged individualist"—and death-denying—society.

But nomads create an illusion of strength. They value freedom, the sense of continual exploration, and the ability to move on without being "tied down" by roots or commitments. As we have seen with both Deidre and Terry, however, this perceived strength can have a stiff price: an inability to commit to staying in a family, a community, a job—the things that provide security, a sense of safety, and belonging. For nomads, there is no anchor and no stability.

If you relate to any of the preceding profiles, you are probably assuming the identity of the nomad. You may be in denial that your loved one has died. You may be avoiding your pain and how it has affected you and those around you. You may no longer trust the world. You may have experienced a genuine trauma, such as Cheryl on September 11, that has not been fairly acknowledged and has shaken your sense of justice. Like Terry, you may have lost your faith in God and may even be very angry at God. You may feel punished but not know why. You may conclude life is so unpredictable that you stop trying to be good or do what's right for you. Although the emotional energy you expend to support these perceptions may help you appear strong, it could very well be counterproductive to true healing.

DISADVANTAGES OF BEING A NOMAD

I view the nomad as a less desirable identity, albeit with some admirable qualities. As you have seen, nomads are the least resolved and actualized of the five identity types. They have not found their place. Although nomads tend to be survivors, their behavior in response to loss is usually reactive rather than proactive. They are most likely to admit to themselves—and even to others—that their work, family, or lifestyle does not fulfill them. They may resort to ways of comforting themselves that are ultimately self-destructive, such as using drugs or getting drunk. They may exhibit other symptoms—depression, anxiety, fear of taking risks, or physical ailments. They have never really figured out what they want in life or how to achieve it.

This is not to say that nomads are always dysfunctional. Many have jobs and careers, families and friends, and even some sense of community. Therefore, they can and do often function normally according to society's standards. But *they are not where they themselves want to be.* They do not have what they want to have and may even undermine their own quest to obtain the very things for which they yearn. They can be in a Catch-22 situation, wandering through life, seeking but not finding what will make them truly happy.

Whether this is due to insufficient time to heal, inadequate support or personal inquiry, or a lack of understanding of what grief is, nomads still face the major challenges of grieving. They must acknowledge and understand how their loss affected their life. They have to accept that their loved one is gone and adjust to a new environment. They must make sense of their loss, evaluate their experience, and find some purpose for their life. Going through the grieving process fully can lead nomads to a new identity and the energy and capacity to reinvest in life. Not doing so will doom them to living a "nomadic" existence. They will not heal.

A cautionary note is warranted here. The grieving process may take quite a long time. In our society, we tend to believe that grieving is a relatively short-term process. Often, as our examples in this chapter have shown, survivors expect to "feel better" in a matter of weeks or months. Others—family members, friends, neighbors, or work associates—also expect them to get back to normal quickly. Although these attitudes are frequently well-meaning, they often have the effect of creating discomfort for mourners that ultimately interferes with healing. Part of the reason is that other people are uncomfortable dealing with death and loss themselves. The commonly held belief is that the sooner we can "forget it and move on," the better everyone will feel.

This myth has been reinforced by the judgments of early researchers on grieving. Dr. Erich Lindemann, a psychiatrist and one of the earliest contributors to understanding grief, had cared for many survivors of the infamous Coconut Grove nightclub fire in Boston in 1943. Hundreds of patrons were trapped and asphyxiated in the rapidly spreading fire. He concluded that the majority of grief reactions could be successfully resolved with eight to ten sessions of psychiatric treatment.[12] Later, Dr. Elisabeth Kübler-Ross, the best-known student of the grieving process, published the results of her research in the groundbreaking book *On Death and Dying* in 1969. She observed that survivors pass through five stages of grief—"denial, anger, bargaining, depression, and acceptance"[13]—in order to move on with their lives. Her book became the gold standard for understanding how we grieve and recover from loss until almost the end of the twentieth century.

Since the 1990s, new research has made several important contributions to our understanding of the grieving process that disagree with the earlier work. We have learned that grieving is highly individualized, not, as Kübler-Ross suggested, a predictable linear emotional path. The "emotional roller coaster" that the bereaved tend to experience early in the mourning process may ease as the death of the loved one becomes more distant. As Steve's story illustrates, however, reminders of their loss can trigger strong emotions in many survivors periodically throughout their lives. Given these new learnings, it appears that Lindemann's "brief treatment" model may be effective *for some people under certain circumstances* but is unlikely to produce long-term healing in the majority of people. Although the pain we feel may be more or less intense at different times, loss echoes throughout our lives.

STRATEGIES FOR HEALING AND GROWTH

As knowledge and experience accumulate, we have also come to recognize that grieving involves more than emotional catharsis. Chapter 1 explains how survivors think differently about the world as well as themselves. Adapting successfully to their loss requires examining an array of beliefs regarding their selfhood, their lives, their relationships, and their spirituality.

If nomads confront their current state of being, they may begin the search for a new and more fulfilling identity. Their lack of an anchor offers them an opportunity to explore the positive aspects of the other identity types. As memorialists, for example, they could choose to honor their lost loved one; as normalizers, they might settle down with a family; as activists, they might become involved in social causes relevant to their loved one's life or death; or as seekers, they might search for spiritual guidance that would provide them with a sense of community.

The following strategies can help nomads evaluate their present status:

1. *Make a commitment to yourself and others*. The key strategy for nomads is to make a commitment to themselves to work through the pain that confronting their grief requires. In order to resolve their continual restlessness, confusion, and grief, nomads must go through the grieving process

as fully and authentically as possible. If you are a nomad, you must come to terms with the fact that you never really resolved your grief—indeed, you may not have gone through a mourning process at all—and that you can no longer avoid it. This means turning *inward*, focusing directly on the past, and making a commitment to confront the unknowns that have allowed you to drift along through life without finding your true purpose. This is the best way for you to move on to the task of finding a new identity that truly works for you.

2. *Don't go it alone.* Seek and accept help in doing your grief work. Your best help might come from your family and friends, especially if they shared the loss with you. Sometimes, however, they are too close to or too remote from your loss to be helpful, and professional assistance would be of greater benefit. Most communities offer many resources to help the bereaved overcome their problems in adjusting to loss. These include clergy, support groups, psychotherapists, and grief counselors. Joining support groups, reading books such as this about others' experiences, and writing a journal to recall memories are activities that have helped some nomads gain insights about their loss and how it has affected them.

Even if your loss occurred many years ago, the guidance of a professional grief counselor or spiritual master may be necessary to exhume memories of a deeply buried past. As Deidre advised: "Keep talking 'til you don't have to talk about it anymore. I didn't do it. People will give you slack, and they will rally around you."

3. *Choose the approach that will help you succeed.* Grief therapy may offer real help to nomads who want to work through their deeply entrenched emotions and beliefs about the world. Because you may have repressed your loss for a

considerable time, like many other nomads, it is important for you to learn how your loss has affected you and then work to adjust to the consequences it has had on how you have lived your life. You need to examine how you feel about yourself, the decisions and choices you have made about how you live, your values and attitudes about life—and death. You may decide to keep some of them; you may adopt new ones as well. You also need to look at how you view the world around you, whether you fit in, whether you trust others.

A holistic approach can help you better understand your loss and grief experience. This involves a comprehensive examination of the physical, social, psychological, spiritual, and philosophical aspects of your life. While it may seem overwhelming, you can set the pace, because working through the grieving experience is an individualized process. The key to success is making a commitment to yourself and others to accomplish your goals.

QUESTIONS FOR FURTHER EXPLORATION

Now that you have read this chapter, you may have already recognized yourself in this identity type; however, take some time to explore your own story more deeply. I encourage you to take the time and space to ponder the following questions. After all, you deserve to know yourself better. This is how you can begin to transform your process towards healing.

These questions may stir you up or upset you. You might ask yourself, "Why should I open up a wound in order to think about and answer questions that are painful?"

As a therapist with many years of experience helping people through the grieving process, I believe that the healing process begins when we're able to assess the ways our past affects our present and future. This process may not be comfortable, but I believe that telling your story with honesty and compassion ultimately leads you to acceptance and peace. You are not bad or deficient for identifying mostly with the nomad, but perhaps there are ways that you aren't living the life you want. I want to help you begin the process of living the productive and meaningful life you deserve. The road to the life you want starts with identifying the beliefs, behaviors, and outcomes that aren't currently in line with your desires and goals.

In order to figure out if this identity type accurately describes you, ask yourself the following questions. Be specific and note examples from your life that support your answers. Don't worry about giving the right answer. These questions are *guidelines* to spark your thinking and to help reveal if this identity type accurately describes you.

1. Do you feel your life really matters or do you find yourself adrift without clear direction? If so, how and why?
2. Do you have difficulty setting goals, both short-term and long-term life goals?
3. If you are able to set goals, are you unable to map out realistic steps toward successful completion? Why?
4. Have you been able to live self-sufficiently in most areas of your adult life? Do you maintain satisfying relationships with friends and loved ones? Are you happy with your work life? How do you relate and connect with others now after losing your loved one?
5. How do you understand the relationship between the loss you experienced and the way you live your life now?

REFLECTIONS FOR THE NOMAD

Telling your story is one of the first ways to heal your unresolved grief. Adjusting to the loss of a loved one is a monumental and profound process. Nomads may have been trying to outrun the direct pain that thinking explicitly about loss may bring up. This process may have protected you from pain that you were not ready to address.

You understand how fleeting life can be, and I want you to enjoy your life. It will require courage and some willingness to feel discomfort as you go through this process, but transforming your grief can help you live the satisfying life that you deserve. With the right support for your needs (a therapist, a support group, intimate friends), you may be safer than you think. Hiding out with your pain may seem like a good solution temporarily, but there may be ways this avoidance is destructive and blocking your happiness.

There are good reasons for you not to want to feel pain, but at this point, there are probably ways that your coping mechanisms are not working in your favor. You are not required to suffer for the rest of your life because of the profound loss you experienced.

Pursuing the strategies suggested in this chapter can allow nomads to choose a more fulfilling identity—as memorialists, normalizers, activists, or seekers. Nomads may be the most fortunate of all the identities, since exploring the advantages and disadvantages of the other identity types can give them the opportunity to truly "reinvent" themselves into the persons they consciously and proactively choose to become.

Three

The Memorialist

> I know of no people for whom the fact of death is not critical, and who leave no ritual by which to deal with it.
>
> —Margaret Mead, anthropologist

WHO ARE THE MEMORIALISTS? Memorialists are survivors whose main goal is to honor their loved one by creating tangible memorials such as rituals, artifacts, and foundations that perpetuate his or her memory. They need to maintain a connection with their loved one by integrating the person into their life through these activities.

Whether the practices are determined by culture, religion, ethnicity, or individual values and beliefs, memorialists have the most powerful desire of all of the identities to honor their loved ones with concrete tributes that bear their name. About one-third of those with whom I spoke were memorialists. The majority were parents honoring their dead children, several were children memorializing their parents, one was a grandmother paying tribute to a grandchild, and several were spouses remembering their husbands or wives.

Memorialists believe, as did Alan Lomax, noted folk traditions and cultural archivist, that "if you lose your past, you lose yourself." He collected and documented traditional music, stories, and other forms of grassroots creativity from America, the Caribbean, and Europe, because his philosophy was that these offer a "window into the human condition."[1]

Maintaining these tangible reminders becomes a priority in their lives. Beginning with the eulogy delivered at the loved one's funeral, memorialists not only preserve memories but also create new ones.

Eulogies honor the dead by expressing gratitude for their life, saying "farewell," and wishing them well on their soul's journey to eternity. According to editor Jill Werman Harris, who compiled a beautiful book of eulogies (and other literary devices) that honor the dead, *Remembrances and Celebrations*, the primary goal of eulogies is to honor the deceased by creating a portrait of their life and their special legacy, which helps those left behind remember them over time.

She points out that eulogies often offer unique benefits to the survivor as well. "Eulogies are a consolatory act. . . . They comfort the bereaved and are enormously cathartic for the eulogist, providing an opportunity to release the powerful emotions brought on by the death of a loved one."[2] Unlike elegies, which are poems that are always mournful, eulogies can make people laugh, convey factual information, or inspire great fervor regarding an issue or cause to which the deceased was committed. Such an example is the final excerpt from the Reverend Ralph D. Abernathy's eulogy of Dr. Martin Luther King Jr.:

> I close by saying what Martin Luther King, Jr., believed: "If physical death was the price he had to pay to rid America of prejudice and injustice nothing

could be more redemptive." And to paraphrase words of the immortal John Fitzgerald Kennedy, permit me to say that Martin Luther King, Jr.'s, unfinished work on earth must truly be our own.[3]

EXAMPLES OF MEMORIAL ACTIVITIES

The scope for memorial activities is as creative and varied as the unique people who conceive them—from photos to gardens, from Web sites to book-length memoirs, from the many war memorials to the Taj Mahal.

Web Sites to Commemorate Loved Ones

Many people have used the Internet as a vehicle for honoring their loved ones. This trend, which began with personal Web sites, has now grown to include a proliferation of specialized sites, for family members, children, and even pets. Write a eulogy, biography, or testimonial; share an anecdote; light a candle; upload photos; and create an album. Family and friends have almost unlimited possibilities for remembering their loved ones. The resources in appendix 2 provide a list of commemorative Web sites.

"Memorial photography" offers families the opportunity to deal with the loss of a newborn and have a token of remembrance. Todd Hochberg, a medical photographer at a Chicago-based hospital, has created images of deceased newborns, baptismal ceremonies, and families praying. A more extreme memento is the "created diamond," called LifeGem, which is a certified, high-quality diamond made through a patented process from the carbon of your loved one. According to an article in the *Washington Post*, this is an "unconventional solution to earthly impermanence."[4]

Public Rituals

Annual memorial services have become traditions for various organizations that serve the dying and their families. Hospices, for example, offer thirteen months of bereavement support for family members of patients they cared for through their deaths. I recall attending beautiful candlelit ceremonies where mourners shared their grief through songs, poems, and testimonials to those who had died during the year. Many attendees appeared each year to honor their deceased and view their names carved in bronze plaques or on marble walls.

Some community-based groups, such as the Wendt Center for Loss and Healing, in Washington, D.C., organize special events, such as the "DC City-wide Homicide Commemorative Event." One of the organizers, who found her twenty-one-year-old son lying shot in the head at their front door, said this of the event:

> [It] allows us the opportunity to share and bring attention to this issue of unsolved murders. So many crimes go unsolved, and people unmentioned. . . . That there are this many people who lost a loved one in a tragedy makes you sad. I just don't want people to forget.[5]

How Different Cultures Honor Their Dead

In Mexico, the culture clearly expresses a sense of connectedness between the past and the present as well as Mexicans' view of life and death. Unlike Americans, who tend to deny the reality of death, Mexicans have an annual holiday to venerate death as a part of life. The "Day of the Dead" is generally a joyous occasion when families and friends of those who have died gather together to share memories and *celebrate,* with dancing and food and song, at the graveside of their loved ones. They decorate the graves with everything from piñatas to clothes to photos—and always flowers, whether an abundant bouquet of lilies from the market or a meager bunch of wildflowers in an old tomato can. For them, these rituals signify a tribute to life, the blessing of death, and the heaven that death delivers. According to Clarissa Pinkola Estés, a Jungian psychologist and storyteller in the Hispanic tradition of the *cantadora,* Mexicans believe that "if *muerte,* death, sits beside you, you are lucky, because you will learn how to live."[6]

In Jewish tradition, family members and friends join the bereaved in the ritual of saying Kaddish, the mourners' prayer, recited many times during the first year after the person's death. As Anne Brener points out in *Mourning and Mitzvah,* "The Jewish calendar recognizes that the ongoing work of mourning is the task of a lifetime."[7] Two rituals, Yizkor and Yahrzeit, are built into the annual commemoration of loved ones who have died. Jews go to the synagogue four times a year to recite the Yizkor prayer, which asks God to remember the soul of the deceased. They also acknowledge each anniversary of the death, Yahrzeit, by lighting a memorial candle at sunset.

When an Irish person dies, it is traditional for the body to be "waked" at home with an open casket rather than at a funeral home (though this is changing). Loved ones stay with the body, keeping vigil and protecting the body until it is buried. Women, and sometimes men, follow a practice of keening, or wailing, accompanied by expressions of affection, usually in Gaelic. Since there is no embalming, burial usually occurs within three days, normally after a funeral Mass. The soul is believed to go immediately to heaven, unless it must first be cleansed of sins in purgatory. On the anniversary of the death every year, called the Day of Memorial, everyone attends a commemorative mass.

Other annual rituals include Grave Sunday, when the community gathers to clean the gravesites and people visit their loved ones, as well as the Catholic holidays of All Saints Day and All Souls Day, celebrated on November 1 and November 2, during which survivors pray for their loved ones' souls.

The Healing Garden

While researching examples of memorialists, I came across a *Boston Globe* article by Eileen McNamara about how the legacies of two individuals had come together to create a living tribute to a woman who had died three years earlier. She wrote:

> For forty years, Bill and Virginia had nurtured over ten acres of wooded hillside around their house, designing rolling lawns, building fishponds and fountains, gazebos and meditation gardens. When his wife passed away after losing her battle with breast cancer, Bill decided the garden could both memorialize her and provide a refuge for women wrestling with the same disease. He donated more than two acres and a small cottage on the property to the Healing Garden, a special program providing services such as massage therapy, yoga, and support groups, to help women coping with breast cancer.[8]

The program was funded by the Lenny Zakim Fund, named after the much-admired Leonard Zakim, former leader of the Anti-Defamation League in Boston and an icon in the community, who himself had died of multiple myeloma in 1999.

THE TYPICAL MEMORIALIST

Perhaps the ultimate example of a memorialist is Shah Jahan, the seventeenth-century Indian emperor whose Taj Mahal was both a tomb and a palace dedicated to his beloved wife, Mumtaz Mahal. Legend has it that after her death in childbirth in 1631, the shah, overwhelmed with grief, determined to perpetuate her memory by building a monument to their eternal love.

Because Mumtaz Mahal was beloved by her people for her benevolence, all of the shah's subjects participated in this extraordinary tribute. More than twenty thousand workers and craftsmen labored for twenty-two years to complete what is now considered one of the most beautiful buildings in the world.

Mumtaz Mahal's white marble mausoleum, encrusted with jewels and decorated with inscriptions from the Koran, is surrounded by a garden symbolizing paradise and canals containing sacred symbols of death, such as cypress trees, fountains, and flower beds—all of which perpetuate forever the memory of the bond of love she and the emperor had shared.

In my research, I found numerous examples of recognition, ranging from charitable foundations, scholarships, and buildings, to artistic endeavors, such as "memory books," songs, sculpture, and gardens that survivors dedicated to their loved ones. These are ways of perpetuating their memory and often of raising awareness of the cause of their deaths as well. For example, in 1980, Nancy G. Brinker promised her dying sister,

Suzy, that she would improve conditions for other women with breast cancer. After her sister passed away, Nancy used her business experience and skills to establish Susan G. Komen for the Cure as a tribute to her sister. This highly successful organization has become a major force in breast cancer fundraising and awareness. It is a living memorial that has been instrumental in improving women's lives.

Public and Private Memorials:
A Grandmother's Story

Memorials such as these may be annual or ongoing rituals shared with relevant public audiences, or they may be private shrines only for survivors and family members. The following story illustrates how the death of an unborn child inspired her young parents to become memorialists by preserving her memory in both ways. They formed a research fund as a public memorial as well as a private garden to aid their personal healing.

Their story was actually told to me by the baby's grandmother, whom I met at a professional meeting. She expressed frustration that her grief, as a grandparent, was not recognized, as if she could not be affected by a "loss once removed." Her explanation was reminiscent of that of the disenfranchised griever described in chapter 2.

Observing that "it is unnatural for parents to outlive their children," she described it as "doubly hard" for a grandparent, who feels helpless at seeing his or her child suffering as well. When her daughter's baby was found to have died in utero due to a rare lung disease, she told me her daughter "had to deliver this dead baby," whom her father named Grace. The infant "was twelve inches long and weighed one pound." The family held and kissed Grace and had her baptized.

To memorialize Grace, her daughter and son-in-law created a backyard garden "loaded with angels." They also established a fund in Grace's name with the American Lung Association as a public memorial that would support research into the unusual disease that had taken her life.

The Relationship between Attachment and Loss

In order to understand memorialists, we must discuss the work of the late British psychiatrist Dr. John Bowlby, a major contributor to theory about the relationship between attachment and loss. For more than thirty years, Bowlby conducted numerous studies of human infants and animals. Foremost among these was his examination of the infant's reactions to separation from its mother. One of his major studies was of young children separated from their mothers during the bombing of London in World War II and the problems that resulted from the separations. He found that these young children were grieving the loss of a key relationship that was critical to their sense of well-being. He concluded that this *attachment behavior* is universal and has the potential to persist throughout life.[9]

The loving bonds created between parent and child early in life provide a sense of security and safety that supports survival. Breaking these attachments causes considerable anxiety and distress. One of Bowlby's many contributions to the study of loss supports the view that the instinctive behavior of attachment is intended to maintain bonds for survival's sake. It also offers a way of understanding the emotional disturbance adults experience when the loving bonds to significant others are broken. Bowlby's analysis was a departure from Freud's classically held belief in the process of decathexis, or separation, of a child from a parent during the child's normal developmental process.

Subsequent researchers Dennis Klass, Phyllis Silverman, and Steven Nickman challenged Freud's proposal because his theory did not apply to separation *by death*. Based on extensive observations of bereaved parents, spouses, and children, these authors found that mourners were developing memories, feelings, and actions that kept them connected to their deceased loved ones and were continuing the relationship rather than letting go.[10] For example, bereaved parents integrated the deceased child into a "part of their inner world"[11] as well as their social reality. People who had lost their wife or husband were found to take on aspects of the deceased spouse or to engage in activities such as regular church attendance that were once generally done only by the deceased.

Furthermore, these altered relationships often evolved over time, comforting survivors and helping them cope with their loss. Rather than sever their emotional bonds with their loved one, these survivors developed a *new* relationship with them, thus continuing their bonds and integrating their loss into a new sense of themselves.

This view contradicted earlier understandings of "holding on" as constituting unhealthy grief. Many researchers affirm the numerous different ways in which the bereaved mourn their loved ones—some healthy, some unhealthy. They do not deny that pathological grieving may occur when mourners refuse to "let go" of their loved one by focusing on the past or denying his or her death. However, if the bereaved live happy, loving, and productive lives, if they acknowledge that their relationship with the loved one has changed, and that *they* have changed, continual healthy growth and adaptation do occur. Incorporating the lost loved one into their

lives, as memorialists do, is an appropriate and healthy way
to grieve.

PROFILES OF MEMORIALISTS

The following five accounts illustrate the unique and various
ways memorialists can honor their loved ones. Memorialists emphasize their value for the past they shared with the
deceased to create living memorials that sustain their loved
ones' memory into the future for their families and their
communities.

Myrim: A Father's Commemoration of His Son

My cousin alerted me to Myrim Baram's work after reading his second book, *My Creations: In Memory of Our Son,
Gabriel Baram*, an impressive compilation of Baram's prolific
and intricate metalworks through photographs, letters, and
tributes he had received in response to his work.[12]

Myrim Baram was an Israeli artist whose metalwork com-
memorates his youngest son, Gabriel (Gavri), who was killed
in the 1973 Yom Kippur War at the age of eighteen. For
more than thirty years after his son's death, Baram applied
his training as a metal artisan to create forty exquisitely
crafted works using bronze, copper, silver, and gold, each with
unique biblical and mythical motifs. He depicted themes of
war, peace, and grief, with images such as doves and olive
branches resting on the globe, the guns and fires of war, and
the scales of justice. He labored for countless hours on each
piece to express his vision.

Many of these commemorative works were Hanukiahs

—candelabras lit for eight nights during Hanukkah, the Jewish Festival of Lights—because Gavri was born during Hanukkah. Baram explained how his son's death affected him:

> The pain is not as strong as it was years ago. My life changed in that I became much more pessimistic. Whereas before the tragedy I was very much devoted to my work in the metal shop—inventing new machines and items—afterwards I devoted my creative talents just to commemorating Gavri's name.
>
> Until today, I cannot accept the loss, cannot resolve the loss ever, but tried to resolve it in continuing with life, both trying to further peace but also commemorating Gavri—give meaning to his short life. My favorite Hanukiah is the very first one I did which has the name "Gabriel" and the "B" for Baram in the background and the symbols of Hanukah. It is the tallest. It is in the main entrance of the Yad LaBanim Institute in Petach Tiqva, where a museum exists to honor soldiers killed from that city.[13]

Baram's beautiful artwork, aesthetically and emotionally moving, has been presented as gifts of peace throughout the world. One magnificent Hanukiah, inscribed with Isaiah's prophecy "Nation shall not lift up sword against nation, neither shall they learn war any more,"[14] was presented to President Bill Clinton for his efforts to promote peace in the Middle East and lit on the first night of Hanukkah in the Oval Office.

Baram received many tributes that eloquently portray his identity as a memorialist, such as the following from the local council president of the kibbutz Baram had helped found:

Myrim chose a unique path to cope with the agony of his tragic loss. His natural talents and his professional skills as a metal artisan equipped him to cope with his loss through creative art. The lights of the Hanukah birthday of his son, Gabriel, are constantly illuminating his father's work. The hanukiot have been on exhibit throughout the world. They represent an artistic experience and demonstrate how sorrow may be contained and become a source for great emotional and mental power and urge to continue life.[15]

As the preceding stories illustrate, the loss of a child violates the natural order of life. Children are not supposed to die before their parents do; parents are not supposed to outlive their children. Regardless of whether the child dies as a baby or an adult, parents lose someone whom they loved and who loved them. The parent-child bond is a unique and irreplaceable relationship.[16]

Such a disruption to one's life narrative is termed a "catastrophic stressor" in the *Diagnostic and Statistical Manual of Mental Disorders*, the manual used by mental health professionals. This is because, when a child dies, parents not only lose a part of themselves but often lose touch with their spouse, their other children, and their assumptions about life as well. They lose their future and the identity that they had created with these assumptions in mind.

Suzanne: Sustaining Her Stillborn Daughter's Memory through Writing

As Margaret Mead discovered, creating rituals is a way to sustain a loved one's memory. Rituals provide survivors with a bridge between the past and the present. Rituals allow survivors to stay connected with their loved ones through their commemorative activities. They offer opportunities for healing, a necessary step in the recovery process. These rituals are often planned around birthdays, holidays, or anniversaries that mark a significant date in the loved ones' lives. For some, the everyday ritual of writing offers solace and comfort. Take Suzanne, an accomplished journalist whom I met at a writers workshop at Kripalu, an ashram in western Massachusetts.

As our group shared the projects we were working on, Suzanne expressed interest in my research. She had lost a baby girl at birth after a normal nine-month pregnancy. Six years later, she still conveyed a sense of shock over her loss. She offered to share with me her writings—poems, newspaper articles, and private reflections—along with her personal account of the stillbirth of her joyfully anticipated daughter, Chloe.

Suzanne told me she'd unexpectedly become pregnant with her second child just as her son was about to enter kindergarten and was initially "ambivalent" about having a baby at the age of forty. Upon learning from the amnio that she was expecting a girl, Suzanne told her mother, who was "so happy" about the news. But her mother, "who had been gravely ill with cancer for five years," soon "took a turn for the worse" and died several weeks later. Following her mother's death, Suzanne said she'd come to think "that [her] daughter would replace [her] mother and [her] relationship with her."

Saying she "sometimes had premonitions," Suzanne pondered the fact that her father-in-law had died two months earlier of Alzheimer's disease and started wondering whether "bad things came in threes." Then, "when Chloe died as well," she said, "I felt I'd never get over it."

As a memorialist, Suzanne commemorated the many anniversaries in that first painful year after her loss by writing regularly. In an article she published in her hometown newspaper describing that first year, Suzanne observed:

> It's been a year of anniversaries. The day I found out I was pregnant. The day I had the amnio and learned she was a healthy girl. The day we chose her name, Chloe. Then, after surgery, the disembodied voice saying "They're working on her." Later, "I'm sorry, Suzanne, we couldn't save your baby." For months after, I dreamt that I was still pregnant. Then came the guilt and shame that my baby had died. Babies aren't supposed to die.[17]

CREATING PRIVATE RITUALS

The guilt and shame Suzanne's words reveal are common emotions for parents who lose infants. She had particular difficulty finding closure after Chloe's death because no explanation was discovered. In search of healing, she continues to write to keep the memories of her daughter alive. One of her annual practices has been to compose a birthday poem for her daughter, such as the one reprinted below, describing life events they might have shared during the year and how her daughter would have grown. These rituals maintain her daughter's presence—even in death—as a part of Suzanne's family.

Chloe's Chimes: Poem to Chloe on Her Seventh Birthday

Angels always hear the perfect chord,
Heaven's metronome is children's feet
Tap dancing on a cloud.
Soft winds blow tiny chimes
That only the sweetness of angels can hear.

Today you would be seven
If you stayed with us on earth.
Last week I gave away your tiny clothes,
And my clothes that held the shape of you.
The scent of lavender faintly clinging to them.

Perhaps you would make your own music,
On the piano or the flute.
You constantly pull the chords around my heart,
Tears fill my eyes that cannot see you.
I can only imagine how your little hands would
Feel in mine, like butterflies or feathers. . . .

I can never give away the memories
In my heart, Chloe, the hopes and dreams I had for you.
The song of love I feel for you.

RESOLVED GRIEF: SUZANNE'S STORY

Suzanne contacted me shortly after she wrote this poem.
She had just returned from Oak Creek in Sedona, Arizona,
where, almost eight years before, she had been pregnant
with Chloe. Sitting by the creek, birdsong filling her ears,
Suzanne wrote me that she felt the presence of Chloe's spirit
amid the rippling waters, tall grasses swaying in the breeze,
sweet-smelling air, and glow of the sun on snow-dusted red
rocks. "A small white feather floated on the water," she
wrote. "I knew then that I left her spirit there. . . . I am at
peace now."

THE DEATH OF A CHILD

It is devastating to parents when their child dies. Child psy-
chotherapist Barbara Rosof describes the stillbirth or sudden
death of a baby as the loss of possibility: for parents, a child

who is stillborn or who dies within days is a distinct and special person.[18] They keep photographs and videotapes, hospital ID bracelets, blankets, tiny T-shirts: the mementos of their children's all-too-brief lives. No matter how short their lives, or how little opportunity their parents had to know them, the children were real and intensely important.

October has been designated as National SIDS, Pregnancy, and Infant Loss Awareness Month for parents to commemorate their precious babies. A Web site at www.october15th.com offers information and ideas to find help and an opportunity to honor them.

Carol and Francaise: Creating a Legacy through Charitable Donations

Creating foundations, charities, and designated funds is a popular way to commemorate the death of a family member and help survivors heal. A number of bereaved parents I spoke with had established scholarship funds in memory of their children. One mother, Carol, set up a scholarship fund at the high school of her son, Peter, after he was killed in an auto crash while traveling to a pregraduation party—the only one of the five boys in the car who died.

Fifteen and a half years after Peter's death, Carol told me proudly that she had also endowed an annual education program for trauma nurses in her son's name at the hospital where Peter was treated and died. Each year the hospital hosts a daylong seminar with an invited panel of experts who discuss the latest trends in trauma nursing. Carol, herself an advanced nurse-practitioner, introduces these sessions by "thanking the nurses for their incredible work and then telling them some funny story [she] recall[s] about Peter."

* * *

Francaise, who lost her eighteen-year-old son, Michael, to a brain tumor ten months after his diagnosis, traveled a bumpy path to find her memorialist identity, eventually establishing a foundation at the university hospital where he had received outstanding treatment.

She described Michael as being a big, tall kid with sparkling eyes whom everyone loved. During the course of his treatment, his long hair had to be shaved and a shunt placed in his head to drain fluid from his brain. He developed seizures and couldn't talk. Unable to swallow, he couldn't even eat any of his favorite dishes that his mother prepared, except for her farfel soup. Although his friends brought him his music and guitar, Michael could no longer do the fingering; others gave him a harmonica, but he couldn't blow.

In Francaise's words: "He was so brave through the whole thing, *supportive of us*. At one point, he said to me, 'It's time for me to move over and make room for another kid.'"

Since Michael had been Francaise's raison d'être, his death, in her words, "changed everything" and left her feeling as if she no longer had anything to do. The challenge of returning to her job and resuming a normal life proved too great. Impulsively, Francaise decided to "escape" to France, giving up her home, her friends, and even her language. During the year and a half she stayed there, she attended an international conference on brain research and decided to raise funds in Michael's name as her "way of connecting with Michael."

Skip: Delaying Grief Until Well After the Loss

Being a memorialist can help people through their grief no matter how or when that grief may appear. Everyone grieves in his or her own way. For some, the full impact of the loss may not be felt until long after the death, as Skip's story shows.

In early 1973, Skip's mother called and told him that his father had been hospitalized with another heart attack and was not expected to live much longer. Skip and his wife immediately flew from their home in New Jersey to Pittsburgh to be with his parents and arrived to find his father in the intensive care unit. The first day Skip visited the ICU, his father looked sick and weak but no worse than Skip had seen him look once or twice before. But when Skip visited his father on the second or third day, he looked gray, the color completely drained from his face. Skip said he'd "never seen him look like that."

That week, Skip and his wife had been planning to travel to New Orleans, where Skip was scheduled to present a paper at a conference. When Skip asked the doctor what he should do about the conference, the doctor said he should go, since his father's death could be days or even weeks away. But on the second night of the conference, Skip and his wife returned to their hotel after dinner with friends to find a message saying that his father had died. Skip quickly found someone else to present his paper and flew back to Pittsburgh for the funeral.

In early 1989, sixteen years to the day after his father's death, Skip found himself unable to sleep. While he lay there in bed thinking about his dad and the last time he saw him, Skip told me he composed a song to his father, finishing it "in tears" after a couple of hours.

Delayed grief can occur for a variety of reasons: Other pressing matters, having to do with the funeral and burial or contacting relatives, may interfere with dealing with the loss. Sometimes the mourner has to "be strong" to hold other family members together and neglects to attend to his or her own needs. Sometimes the support system the mourner thought would be there isn't.

When a grief reaction appears years later, it can sometimes be attributed to a "trigger" or reminder of the loved
one—the anniversary of the death, the death of someone
else or even a pet, or a flash of memory that is associated
with the loved one. In these cases, survivors reexperience
the loss, as they might have at the time of the death, with
symptoms of acute grief, such as numbness, sadness, confusion, and changes in sleep or appetite. The response is likely
to reflect the way the person has typically responded to other
losses, as we discuss below.

Gender Differences in Grieving

In the last few years, many experts, including researchers Terry
Martin and Kenneth Doka, have determined that people
grieve in different ways. The conventional wisdom, supported
by research, has been that grieving *requires* emotional expression, since grief is *emotional energy* in response to loss. Martin
and Doka, however, have identified two major types of grievers, which they call "intuitive" and "instrumental."[19] Intuitive
grievers feel the painful feelings and give vent to them by crying and sharing with others. They express their emotions and
are most likely to seek help from grief counselors or support
groups. They conform to the common understanding of how
people grieve. Since women tend to be more expressive emotionally than men, I am sure it comes as no surprise to you that
most women are intuitive grievers.

In contrast, instrumental grievers, such as Skip, temper their
pain. They respond more often by attempting to solve problems,
and *think* rather than *feel* through their experience. Thus, they
direct their psychic energy toward "doing" things. Instrumental grievers see themselves as taking care of their loved one by
performing activities such as settling the estate or taking over
the family business. These concrete tasks allow the mourners

to problem-solve and maintain control of themselves and their environment, thereby creating a sense of normalcy and security that supports their achieving resolution of their grief.

This form of grieving is attributed more often to men than women in American society. Males are socialized at a young age to suppress their feelings of fear, insecurity, and especially sadness. They aren't supposed to cry, because these displays are perceived as a sign of weakness. As a consequence, boys learn to behave rationally, to express themselves through activity, to solve problems, to complete tasks. Therefore, we can conclude that instrumental grieving among men is a perfectly logical response to loss.

Resolving Grief: A Sense of Completion

For many years, as his wife, Judy, observed, Skip coped with his father's death by "diverting his attention to work, tennis, and physical exertion generally." While Judy expressed considerable frustration with his behavior at the time, Skip's response was actually an effective adaptive strategy for those who tend to process events cognitively rather than through intense feelings.

Skip is a talented musician, who has played in several musical groups and also composes music. It was natural, then, for him to express his love for his father through his music. He ultimately honored his father's death and preserved his memory by writing a song, "I Never Said Goodbye." Such tributes are the hallmark of the memorialist.

I Never Said Goodbye

I never said goodbye. I never said goodbye.
They'd saved your life so many times before.
I thought they'd do it just once more.

And still I don't know why.
I let you go without a last goodbye.
And still I don't know why.
I let you go without a last goodbye.

I never said goodbye. I never said goodbye.
Those things I wish I said so long ago
I wish that somehow you could know.
I wonder if you knew.
I never told you how much I loved you.
I wonder if you knew.
I never told you how much I loved you.

I never said goodbye. I never said goodbye.
And now I've got two children of my own.
It won't be long before they're grown.
I've always tried to be
The kind of dad for them that you were for me.
I've always tried to be
The kind of dad for them that you were for me.

ADVANTAGES OF BEING A MEMORIALIST

After the death of their loved ones, memorialists have chosen a new identity, devoting themselves to keeping alive the memory—and the meaning—of their relationship with their loved ones. Memorialists appreciate that life is finite, that living for the moment is precious as a reminder of what has happened in the past. They view their relationship to the world and their priorities through their family, friends, and home. These values have the effect of institutionalizing the memory of their loved one's life and helping the survivors come to terms with their grief.

POTENTIAL DISADVANTAGES OF BEING A MEMORIALIST

Memorialists can hold on to the past in ways that prevent them from continuing with their own lives. Incorporating a loved one into oneself and maintaining the bonds with that person may become an obsession, an emotional block. Memorialists may fear that their loss will leave them with a tremendous sense of isolation and even abandonment. It may actually lead to depression and an inability to function productively.

I found that some memorialists tend to retain their ties to anything and anyone who reminds them of their lost loved one. This attitude can hinder them from reaching out, exploring new options, adapting to their environment, and potentially developing another identity.

There are, for example, widows who still see themselves as married women, don't appreciate the potential benefits of being single and independent, and are not open to opportunities to meet someone new. A famous case in point is Queen Victoria, who ruled the British empire for more than sixty years with her first cousin, Prince Albert, by her side. Their intense marriage produced nine children. In "The Legacy of Loss," Monica McGoldrick describes how the queen descended into a deep depression following the death of her beloved Albert:

> For 40 years she wore mourning dress in the style of the year her husband died. . . . She developed an obsession

with cataloging everything, so that nothing would be changed. She surrounded herself with mementos of the past and gave orders that nothing would ever be thrown away—there were to be no further changes or losses. As long as she lived these orders were obeyed.[20]

STRATEGIES FOR HEALING AND GROWTH

The key strategy for memorialists is to find ways to preserve the memory of their loved ones in order to provide meaning for their own lives as they move forward. Memorializing the past while also moving forward requires a delicate balance, however. The stories I have presented in this chapter offer numerous ideas for how to accomplish this.

If the memorialist identity resonates with you and you feel that finding some way to memorialize your loved one would promote your healing and growth, you may wish to review your memories of your loved one, consult with others about their memories and perceptions of him or her, and consider what might be a meaningful way in which to honor them. For example, think about what was important in your loved one's life. How did she spend her time when she wasn't with you? Did she enjoy beauty, art, music? Was she into sports and other kinds of physical activity? Did he spend his leisure time seeking knowledge or traveling to far-off places? Was it important for him to create opportunities for others to achieve their dreams?

In the process of drawing that portrait, ask others to share their thoughts and recollections of your loved one in various contexts, such as work, school, and community. Finally, seek out other survivors who share your experience, especially those who have chosen to memorialize their loved ones in some way.

Many memorialists need the support of people who knew the person who died, whereas others need the company of strangers who have experienced a similar kind of loss.

There are general bereavement groups as well as groups organized by kinds of losses, such as sudden death, cancer, or terrorism. Other examples are Compassionate Friends, for parents who have lost a child, and many local support groups for those who have lost spouses or partners. There are even more specialized bereavement groups for those who have lost a baby or for those who have lost a loved one by suicide. There are groups for young widows and widowers, or those who have lost a lifelong companion.

Because memorialists may experience a protracted mourning process, they can feel especially isolated in their grief and feel as if no one else has experienced what they have. The more closely memorialists identify with other survivors, hear their stories, and understand that they are not isolated, the more likely it is that they will be able to find a meaningful place in their life for their loved one. The realization that they are not alone and that others understand their pain is a comfort in itself. By identifying with other survivors of loss, the bereaved can feel free to reinvest in creating a new future for themselves.

In addition to support groups, information through pamphlets, books, and the Internet can dispel the sense of despair an unresolved memorialist feels. Once the barrier is broken, memorialists can choose a new way of viewing their loss that allows them to honor their loved one without holding themselves back from finding a fulfilling meaning and purpose for their own lives.

Consider what creative talents and ideas you might apply

to the preservation of your loved one's memory. Use your interests, passion, and talent for writing, painting, songwriting, even gardening to remember the happy aspects of your loved one. How can you convert these interests into a permanent memorial for him or her?

By reading this chapter, you may have already recognized yourself as a memorialist; however, it is worthwhile to explore your own story more deeply. As I said earlier, reviewing your story is part of finding your own path to healing.

QUESTIONS FOR FURTHER EXPLORATION

Are you most like the memorialist?

1. List the concrete ways you remember your lost loved one. How have you memorialized your loss in creative and special ways? For example, have you written something, a poem, essay, or eulogy about your loved one? Have you created a charity or foundation in your loved one's name? Have you organized something, such as a memorial walk or run or a training program?

2. Have your acts of remembrance allowed you to stay connected with your loved one? Do you see this act of continuity in relationship to your grief? In other words, has the memorializing act played a role in helping you heal?

3. Are there hidden ways that you remember your loved one that aren't visible to others or even to yourself? What are the unconscious ways you stay connected to your lost loved one? Are there any ways that your connection and loyalty to your loved one do not serve your best interests, and are detrimental to your happiness? How and why?

4. What do you imagine your lost loved one would think, say, or feel about the ways you've memorialized their life? Write an appreciation letter to yourself from your loved one imagining their reaction to the projects you created in their honor.
5. How do you understand the relationship between the loss you experienced and the way you live your life now? Are you comfortable with your memorialist identity?

REFLECTIONS FOR THE MEMORIALIST

Using your talent and creativity to maintain your connection with the loved one you lost is a productive way to create meaning from your loss. Your loved one is not far from memory and is not forgotten because you honor your beloved with acts of remembrance. Exploring your abilities, interests, and creativity in ways that you, your loved ones, and your lost loved one can appreciate can be helpful and allow you to remain connected to your loved one in a meaningful and healthy way.

Reflecting on the questions above may allow you to recognize all the creative ways you have processed your loss. There may be things you've done that you haven't recognized as acts of the memorialist. Even putting together the funeral program or writing an obituary are fulfilling ways to memorialize your loved one.

Are there any ways you've wanted to remember your loved one that you don't feel you have permission to do? I give you permission now.

Four

The Normalizer

> To be rooted is perhaps the most important and least recognized need of the human soul.
> —Simone Weil, French philosopher, from *The Need for Roots*

WHO ARE THE NORMALIZERS? Normalizers are the survivors whose primary goal is to create or re-create the life they lost when their loved one died. The greatest number of people who told me their stories found their new identity as normalizers. They fell into three categories: (1) spouses who were seeking to remarry, (2) adult children whose families had been disrupted by the death of a parent or sibling and who wanted to create or re-create the family life they had lost, and (3) family members who reconciled after confirming the death of a loved one.

Examples include a number of widows and widowers who had been happily married and chose to remarry. Also, several parents who had lost a child decided to adopt or have another natural child. Ever mindful of the impact of their loss, normalizers value their relationships with others, especially family and friends, and they are focused on making the most of their time on earth. They have learned that life is finite and unpredictable, yet precious.

THE TYPICAL NORMALIZER

In my research, I found a striking example of the normalizer in the story of Georgia Nucci, who had lost her two teenage children in 1988 in separate tragedies within a year.[1] Her eighteen-year-old daughter, Jennifer, died within weeks after contracting hepatitis while on an exchange program in Ecuador. While Nucci was still grieving, her son, Christopher, who had been spending his junior year abroad studying in England, was killed in the terrorist bombing of Pan Am Flight 103 over Lockerbie, Scotland.

These dual losses devastated Nucci, who turned to the organization formed by survivors, Victims of Pan Am Flight 103, to advocate for improvements in airline procedures during disasters. She became active in this organization and also created a book of profiles to preserve the memories of all those lost to the terrorist bombing.

Nonetheless, Georgia and her second husband, Tony, continued to feel "a loss that filled them not just with sadness but also with anger and defiance."[2] She continued:

> As a consequence of terrorism, I was no longer a mother. I wanted to regain my status as a mother. Terrorism wasn't going to have another victim in me. On what would have been Christopher's twentieth birthday [a little over a year later], we decided we wanted to adopt a child.[3]

As an older couple, the Nuccis were not high on the priority list of American adoption agencies. However, they persisted in their desire to adopt and explored other options. They learned about the forty thousand children around the world who were abandoned every day. Through a friend, they connected with an orphanage in Bogotá, Colombia, which sent them a photograph of four brothers and sisters who had been deserted by their mother two years earlier. They could not resist.

Less than two years after their tragedies, the Nuccis were the proud parents of a new family of two boys and two girls, ages four to twelve. As the children adjusted to their new parents and their safe and comfortable home, they heard stories of their "older brother and sister," which integrated the deceased children into their memories and their life as a family.

PROFILES OF NORMALIZERS

Normalizers have lost a member of their family, and sometimes the entire family, whether this involves the physical loss of several members, or the symbolic sense of family. The following stories illustrate how normalizers grieve and reinvest in the world with a renewed commitment to what they most missed and valued.

Elizabeth: Before Death, Reconciliation

Elizabeth, a brilliant, beautiful young woman of thirty-three, recalled her mother's death ten years earlier at the age of fifty-four, following a two-and-a-half-year bout with colon cancer. After graduating from the college her mother had wanted her to attend, not the one Elizabeth would have preferred, Elizabeth had fled the controlling environment her mother had created. She moved far away to Japan, where she worked as a model and teacher for several years.

When her father first contacted Elizabeth to inform her, "Mom has cancer," she rushed home to join her father, brother, and mother. After her mother recovered from surgery to remove part of her colon (the oncologist assured the family that "they got it all"), Elizabeth spent time with her mother. She and her mother traveled to the Colorado mountains, where they skied together and enjoyed the outdoors they both cherished. Grateful for their time together, Elizabeth returned to Japan. Her mother suffered a recurrence of her disease, however, and died a few months later.

Though Elizabeth felt some guilt about not being present when her mother died, she felt resolved about their relationship because they had been able to reconcile before her death.

Martha: Making Peace

Another individual who was able to make peace before her loved one passed away was Martha, a successful and ambitious woman who, at fifty-three, had never been close with her mother. When the family learned that her mother was terminal, dying of metastatic colon cancer, Martha became frustrated with her stoic, Episcopalian relatives, who just wanted to "wait it out." Martha, who needed to respond more actively, assumed the role of her mother's primary caregiver. This gave Martha an opportunity to develop an intimacy with her mother that she had not experienced before. She talked with her mother about what life meant to her. They asked each other for forgiveness. Martha assured her mother of her life's positive impact. When her mother could no longer speak, tears flowed down her mother's cheeks. Minutes later, she died.

Martha recalls that going through the dying process with her mother made her realize that "you can't procrastinate." You need to take risks and get up the courage to do whatever is important to you because "you may not have another chance."

The experience of attending to her dying mother was so profound that Martha soon resigned from a high-powered position in a retail business to be with her husband and fifteen-year-old son. "What's really important is my family," she explained.

I asked Martha, "What lessons did you take away from your experience with your mother?" Without hesitation, she answered: "To make time one-on-one with those you love. To help others in the family deal with their loss. Slow down. Talk. Listen. Empathize."

Octavia: One Happy Marriage Leads to Another

Octavia is a charming woman who had left her native England for California to earn her doctorate in anthropology and landed in Washington, D.C., years later with a PhD. She had an appealing British accent; a wonderful, droll sense of British humor; and a laugh to match. When I observed her from a distance one night in a popular Chevy Chase restaurant, enjoying a glass of Chardonnay with a tall, distinguished gray-haired gentleman, they were both laughing continually throughout their conversation, and I thought to myself: "This is the one she's been waiting for!"

Only a few months later, Octavia and Ron were married in a lovely home ceremony surrounded by family and friends. "He made me laugh," Octavia explained. She had been unable to resist him. When Ron died of a massive stroke just three and a half years later, Octavia was devastated.

She told me it had been her first marriage (at the age of fifty) and Ron's second. Octavia quickly became very fond of Ron's close family, including his two grown children, and his many good friends. As Ron's health gradually deteriorated in the two years preceding his death, he maintained what Octavia termed "an irreverence" that she found both endearing and frustrating. His "quick and painless" death left her "exhausted but relieved."

Octavia described returning to the single life as "horrible." As a new widow, she felt insecure, judged by others, and relegated to a lower rung on the social ladder. She realized that some of the couples with whom she and Ron had been friendly no longer wanted to be around her. As she observed succinctly, "You find out who your true friends are." She did not become bitter, though, saying that she "loved being married to my husband," who had taught her a lot about relationships and about life. Thanks to Ron, Octavia had learned "to be able to look at things objectively and to make the best of things."

Now Octavia lives in the present, accepting the realities of life as they arise. She participates in a Jungian therapy group that is discussing the Holy Grail, learning that life is a journey and that the meaning of life is to learn, to give to others, to participate in a community of people. She views life's challenges as a mix of ups, downs, and lonely periods, observing that, ultimately, "it's about relationships." In particular, she maintains a continuing relationship with Ron's supportive family, which she says she values "enormously." Octavia sums up her experience by saying that she remains hopeful, adding, "I feel blessed to have had the experience, the memories. . . . I'd love to be married again one day."

As a normalizer, Octavia's priorities include marriage, family, friends, and community. These preferences exemplify what motivates her to re-create her positive marital experience. As of this writing, Octavia has remarried and is living happily in Maryland with her new husband.

Carl: Creating as an Adult the Family Life That He Lost in Childhood

Other normalizers wish to create a life that they had hoped for but had not fully achieved. When a prominent dentist in the community died suddenly of a heart attack, he left behind his wife; an eighteen-year-old daughter, Helen; and three sons, aged ten, fourteen, and sixteen. Helen explained that following her father's death, the community seemed to have no idea how to respond to the death or how to treat her family. Not only did her father's friends and associates stop calling, but she and her mother and brothers were no longer invited to participate in family events. In her words, "Whatever had been normal in our lives went down the drain with my father's death." The sense of being ostracized prompted one of her brothers to observe angrily that the family had gone from "riches to rags."

This story illustrates how members of the same family can react very differently to a single death and develop very different identities in response to it. Helen, who was a freshman in college at the time, pursued a path that led her to find meaning as a seeker, an identity I discuss in chapter 6. Helen's brother Carl, who was fourteen when their father died, made choices that led him to a normalizer identity.

Sitting in the comfortable sunroom in the beautiful home he and his wife had built, Carl shared his story. He said that he'd had a close relationship with his father, whom he "idolized," and that they'd done many things together: skiing, sailing, building a boat. Carl admitted that for many years, he refused to acknowledge the death and imagined that his father would be coming back. In retrospect, Carl thinks that if he'd been given an opportunity to see his father dead, it might have helped him accept the finality of his loss much sooner.

Carl felt that the primary effect of his father's death was "to make me grow up right away." He started working at the age of fourteen and felt forced to become self-sufficient because his mother "couldn't handle things." In the wake of his father's death, his mother's decisions left Carl's family "financially deprived," lacking what Carl termed "the security that children expect to have from their parents."

Carl seemed to realize that he needed support and male role models. He sought the guidance of some Episcopal priests and received life-sustaining support from them. A friend's father taught Carl how to drive and let him use the family's car, even though Carl's friend wasn't allowed to.

What Carl said he misses most was not being an adult with his father. Apologizing to me for "being emotional," he explained that he "never got to have a beer with [his] father or do fun things together." Carl felt the absence of his father's support especially keenly while he was raising his own children, who "grew up without a grandfather." Carl termed the loss of his father "a rip-off for me."

When Carl married, he vowed to create a stable and secure life for his family with a wife who would be an equal partner, who could take care of their children if anything happened to him. Living in southern Maine near where he grew up, Carl and his wife have created what many would perceive as a "model family," with two highly accomplished children and a large presence in their community. "I look forward to doing things with my kids as adults, being a grandparent, helping them to develop the confidence I didn't have, because I am there to support them."

Carl acknowledges that he still mourns his father, almost thirty years later. He believes that his father's death strongly affected the choices he made for his life; his values, priorities, and worldview; and the person he is today.

William: Delaying Grief by Numbing the Pain

I met William in a Barnes & Noble café to interview him. Though I had been a close friend of his older sister for more than twenty years and William and I had crossed paths many times through her, we had never talked about how his father's death had affected him until I approached William directly. At forty-something, he had finally married about eight years ago and had a six-year-old son, whom he and his wife adored. Working in the family's highly successful business, he seemed to have attained the stability and security that normalizers value, though his journey illustrates a "bumpier" process than Carl's.

William's father had died suddenly when he was just sixteen months old. With their undeveloped capacity for memory, infants and toddlers experience little immediate impact of loss, though family disruption, such as parental and sibling dysfunction, can interfere with their adjustment. By the time they reach school age, however, children have a sense of themselves in comparison to others.

William recalls becoming aware that he had no father when at the age of seven he went to parents' day with his mother. He said he didn't lack for male role models, though, since his friends' fathers looked out for him and his mother arranged for him to have a Jewish Big Brother. William also "had lots of family around," including an uncle and a grandfather who took William to ball games. According to William, "I felt special because people felt sorry for me, and I bought into their pity for me."

Since William's mother worked and was able to provide him with the means to go to summer camp and do other things that his friends were doing, he wasn't made to feel underprivileged. William summed it up as a "normal childhood" and remarked that "in those years, I didn't feel a loss."

For school-age children, having other relatives and adult role models can supply many of the children's basic needs for emotional support, love, companionship, and financial help.

Despite these supports, however, when William was close to finishing high school, things started to spiral. His mother was hospitalized numerous times for diabetic shock and depression, which she had experienced intermittently since her husband's unexpected death. His two older sisters were away at college, leaving him home alone to care for his mother. To escape, he often took his mother's car, although that made him feel guilty. He turned to experimenting with drugs and self-medicating to "block things out of [his] life." As he explains, "I got by because I was smart, but I didn't do much work."

His pattern of using drugs and underachieving continued even after he surprised his family by graduating from college "on time." William shared similarities with many whose grief, like that of the nomads, remains unresolved. He never talked about his father and did a "good job of suppressing" his thoughts about him. He didn't know what career he wanted to pursue, so he dabbled in architecture, design, and urban planning. He described himself as "slumming along in lots of jobs." Finally, he "fell back" to various management positions in the retail liquor business, where he had considerable experience, and stabilized his career. He had a hard time, however, sustaining relationships with women, because he "didn't want anyone to get too close." Seeing his sisters moving on with their lives and families made William feel worse about his own life.

When he was forty, William finally met the woman who was to become his wife and settled into a normal family life—a home, a beautiful son, and steady work as a manager in the family-owned business. Although he remains close to his two older sisters and many former college friends, William continues to alleviate his pain by using various substances—cigarettes, alcohol, even marijuana. "I am very self-destructive," he admitted.

Moving toward Resolution

While William now understands that his substance use helps him block out painful experiences, he is still struggling with how losing his father affected him. This behavior has created tensions in his marriage, but it has also motivated him to seek professional help and explore self-help methods for changing. William is now on the path to recovery, propelled by his desire to hold on to the family he created and through which he finds his identity as a devoted husband and father.

According to Neil Chethik, author of *FatherLoss: How Sons of All Ages Come to Terms with the Deaths of Their Dads*, men who grew up without their fathers have missed the "close-up view of the beast he would become one day: a man."[4] Chethik recounts the memories of hundreds of men who reminisced about the power of their father's handshake, his height and size, riding piggyback high on his shoulders, and feeling so protected. He discusses how these sons experience paternal affection not as hugging, kissing, or holding as it is typically defined but as wrestling, tossing a ball around, or what Chethik calls "*loving attention by a father toward his son.*"[5] He offers a useful prescription for men such as William:

The man who grew out of the boy had to finish his mourning in adulthood, identifying the legacies of

the loss in his life, addressing disruptive behavior patterns, and finding a way not to banish the memory of
his father but to settle it, gracefully, within himself.[6]

Tina: Family Reconciliation after a Crisis

Sometimes the experience of losing someone we love has a
way of bringing families together. One of the most prevalent
reasons is that people realize that life can be short and that
relationships, especially with those to whom we are connected by blood and history, are important and sometimes
irreplaceable. Sudden death from accidents, heart attacks,
and other unanticipated events can create the circumstances for reconciliation of family members who may have
been estranged for years.

When American Airlines Flight 11 hit the North Tower
of the World Trade Center, one of the building's largest ten-
ants was Cantor Fitzgerald, L.P., a leading financial services
provider, whose headquarters occupied the 101st through
105th floors. Although its headquarters was eight to twelve
floors above the plane's impact, it would soon be determined
that Cantor Fitzgerald suffered the greatest loss of life—658
employees—which affected a total of 800 families and 950
children.

Tina's thirty-nine-year-old nephew Ron, her brother's son,
was a managing partner at Cantor Fitzgerald. She quickly
realized that Ron might be in his 104th-floor office. Living
in the Boston area, Tina and her niece were close, though
she had been distanced from her brother and sister-in-law for
many years. Like many people who need to know whether
their family members are safe in a time of crisis, Tina gathered
her niece, three daughters, and elderly parents together and
drove to her nephew's home in Greenwich, Connecticut, to

await word from him. There, they tried to feel purposeful by cooking continually throughout their vigil, until the end of the week, when they came to terms with the reality that "he wasn't coming back." Two weeks later, a memorial service was held, and, as Tina explained, at that point, "everything changed."

Her brother and sister-in-law, who had been living in retirement in Florida, returned to New England and built a house close to where their daughter lived, anticipating their joyous role as grandparents. They named their home "The Inn" as an invitation to visitors, including Tina and her family. Acknowledging the unpredictability of life, Tina and her sister-in-law bonded for the first time. Ron's parents now devote much of their time to preserving their son's memory through various memorializing activities, including charitable events and supporting a scholarship established by his high school friends, an annual road race, and a walk.

Nonetheless, Tina believes that as a result of her nephew Ron's death, the overriding choices her brother and sister-in-law made reflected their newfound priority of being together as a family. As a tribute to their son's memory, Ron's parents made an effort to restore damaged relationships, which has brought healing not just to them but also to the entire family.

When Survivors Don't Grieve

Sometimes we do not mourn someone we were "supposed to love" and instead experience other thoughts and feelings toward the deceased. A very dear and thoughtful friend who was aware of my research on the long-term impact of grief e-mailed me about her grown daughter's reactions to her father's death six months before. She indicated that her daughter had expressed guilt for "not yet shedding a tear" and observed that her daughter "is not likely to go through the death-grief-reconciliation-identity process." By way of explanation, my friend described the father as

> a completely self-absorbed, self-oriented [man] . . . who used money as his "currency" for extracting love from his children. . . . My daughter repressed her knowledge and her true feelings regarding all of this. . . . Whereas she thought she was going to be bereaved and grieving on the surface, her deeper feelings were those of a long-held self-protective disconnect from this man, who was hurting and rejecting, yet loving and superficially a "good" man.

There are many reasons why people do not express grief. As we saw in chapter 3, overt grief, through emotional response, is not the only way to grieve. But my friend's daughter was experiencing a different reaction. It was not that she did not *express* grief but that she did not *feel* grief. The typical feelings of sadness and confusion were absent. Even anger toward her father seemed to be missing.

Although we tend to idealize the concept of family and assume that all families are loving, comforting, and accepting, many people find that this image falls far short in reality. Writer Victoria Secunda recounts the "difficult history" she had with her mother from the moment of her birth. Before she died at eighty-two, her mother conveyed the lifelong message of her feelings about her oldest daughter: "Don't tell Vicky," she instructed Vicky's younger sister, Nancy. She did not want Vicky to attend her funeral.[7]

The nature of the relationship correlates closely with how —and whether—the survivor grieves. As grief scholar Dr. William Worden suggests, "The intensity of grief is determined by the intensity of love."[8] If, as the above examples show, the relationship was fraught with rejection, pain, and conflict, the survivor may not experience the end of the relationship as a loss. He or she might actually feel relief.

Research has shown that when a person is severely abused, or traumatized by various forms of violence, *repression*—burying memories so deep that the victim doesn't recall them—can actually be healthy. A complete "letting go" may also be considered a healthy coping response. Many Holocaust survivors suppress excruciating memories because recalling them could hinder their ability to function. Some relationships *are* toxic.

Jeanne: From Toxic to Tender—Finding the Loving Mother She Never Had

When I first met Jeanne, I was struck by her high energy and infectious laugh. An attractive redhead with bright green eyes and long lashes, she had a smile that radiated warmth and vivacity, and she conveyed this aura with clients and colleagues alike. As vice president of a leading career management firm that helps companies and their employees through often-painful layoffs, Jeanne managed and delivered the training programs and workshops that teach job-search skills, such as interviewing and networking. Although Jeanne is definitely a "people person," her outgoing manner masks the internal sensitivity she still feels about her mother's unexpected death thirty-seven years ago.

Jeanne vividly recalled how her mother had died of a sudden heart attack at the age of forty-four, on the weekend of Jeanne's thirteenth birthday. Her mother had gone to bed with a cold. But when her father went to check on her at 7:30 that evening, she heard him cry out in a panic:

"Martha, wake up!" Then the ambulance came to take her mother away, and before it reached the hospital, she was pronounced dead. When her father returned the next morning, his six children, aged five to eighteen, were waiting for him to drive them to school. Surrounded by their grandmother, who lived downstairs, close aunts, and neighbors, they were all crying, stunned by this young woman's death. As Jeanne described it, "The funeral was not real morbid. We were in too much shock to realize what happened. Afterwards, we were embraced by everyone taking care of us, since my mom was very sociable, enjoyed parties, and had lots of friends."

Even in the midst of the shock and the tears of relatives and friends, Jeanne's reaction to her mother's death was not typical of most children who lose their mothers. Jeanne explained that she had "never connected emotionally" with her mother, who had "picked on" her and made her feel she "wasn't pretty or cute." Jeanne said she had "few memories of her being a mother to me." Instead, Jeanne's memories included "coming home from the third grade and making her [mother] highballs." She observed that "if Mama was in a good mood today, it was probably because she was drinking. When she was in a bad mood, forget it." Jeanne's brother tried to laugh off the situation, her sisters refused to acknowledge it, and her father sought refuge in his work when her mother "ranted and raved."

We often assume that a loss must be devastating to those left behind. If conflict existed when the person died, if feelings go unresolved, or if reaction to the loss is denied, delayed, protracted, or in some way distorted, what is called "complicated mourning" may ensue. In Jeanne's case, however, the loss may have been experienced as a sense of release and relief. At thirteen, she rationalized that since her mother was sick with alcoholism, God had taken her and they would be better off without her. Noted psychologist and specialist in children's grief Phyllis Silverman discusses the capacity of children at different stages of development to respond to death. Adolescents such as Jeanne, she says, are able to "articulate their need for continuity and stability"[9] and seek ways to order their lives.

Jeanne's family seemed to exemplify the response Silverman describes. A close friend of Jeanne's noted that after the death of Jeanne's mother, "Your household didn't skip a beat." The five girls shared housekeeping responsibilities, while their father cooked, took the family to church on Sundays, instituted a family tradition of having Sunday dinners together, and just generally "made sure [the children] were loved and safe." Jeanne described her mother's and father's roles in her life like this: "I loved my father, because I had a sense of safety with him. He had always protected me against my mother's meanness. So, when she died, I didn't miss her."

Jeanne found other mothers to take care of her. She visited an aunt every weekend, and as her friendship with her best friend developed in her teens, Jeanne told me that "her [friend's] mother mothered me." Now, as an adult, Jeanne has developed strong relationships with her nieces and nephews, who call her "Auntie" and allow her to fulfill her maternal instincts by caring for them. Her four sisters have criticized Jeanne for being "needy," and to this day, she cannot talk about their mother with them. Is it a sign of weakness to acknowledge your innermost need to be mothered? Jeanne doesn't think so. "I must have needed it because I welcomed it."

PJ: Multiple and Traumatic Losses

As devastating as it is to experience the death of a loved one, living through more than one loss is unthinkable. Consider the impact when these losses are parents of young children and teenagers or when their deaths are the result of unusual or violent circumstances. Compound this with the loss of a lifelong relationship, a sibling.

When PJ and I first met while working together on a project at a community college, I could not have imagined the journey she had been traveling. PJ was competent and well regarded, her sense of humor quite apparent as she mingled with other committee members. Later, when she offered to share her story, I was moved by her composure and insight, and the choices she had made for her own life.

During the U.S. polio epidemic in the late 1950s, her mother had contracted polio while pregnant with PJ, who was "born in an iron lung." At the time, doctors held out little hope for the survival of either mother or child. Yet PJ's mother had a fierce will to live and actually survived for four more years, until her death at the age of thirty-eight. PJ "remembers" her mother only through the memories of her older siblings. Her own recollections are of having "a very unhappy childhood," during which she "cried a lot [and] was very quiet and withdrawn."

PJ described her father, a prominent surgeon, as "a tragic figure." Although his four children—aged twelve, ten, six, and four at the time of their mother's death—could tell that he loved them, he suffered from depression and alcoholism and had difficulty expressing his emotions. When he remarried seven years later, his new wife fit the mold of what PJ terms "the classic stepmother from hell." The woman "exploited [her father's] position in the community to climb the social status ladder while manipulating and trapping [the children] at home."

Despite these problems, PJ described her teen years as happy. She excelled in high school with little parental or adult guidance, aiming to please her father and gain his attention. Describing herself as a "really good Catholic girl, a people-pleaser," she enjoyed the company of friends, boyfriends, and an especially close relationship with her older sister, Carrie, whom she said "helped [her] through it." During her senior year, however, her father's alcoholism caught up with him. His medical colleagues could no longer cover for him and sent him to rehab for treatment. PJ recalled that he seemed to get his act together and appeared happier. She graduated as class valedictorian. That evening, she achieved her goal when he took her for a walk and expressed how proud he was of her.

THE TRAUMA OF SUICIDE

The next morning, PJ awoke to the news that her father had shot himself. Thirty years later, as she related her story to me, the racing thoughts and raw emotions of her father's suicide still welled up in her. As the last person to have seen her father alive, she "felt tremendous guilt," wondering whether she could somehow have made him happy and thereby prevented his death. Because PJ, the youngest child, had just graduated from high school and was poised to go off to college, it occurred to her that her father might have "*planned it*" all along, figuring that since PJ "didn't need him anymore," he had "finished his job and could kill himself."

At the time, however, PJ's reaction was muted. After working and preparing all summer, she went off to college and had "a great first year." But in her sophomore year, she had a nervous breakdown, an intense grief reaction to her father's death. This time, instead of guilt, she felt rage toward her father, and intellectually she felt "cathartic" at expressing it. But she also turned that anger on herself. She began drinking, drugging, and acting out sexually, all self-abusing behaviors. The intensity of her guilt also surfaced, as she imagined herself responsible for the deaths of both her parents. She was compelled to leave school in New York and went to live with her sister Carrie in Boston. Following a year of continued disruption, PJ entered therapy and, after more than a year, was able to return to college and complete her degree.

When a person experiences multiple losses, especially in childhood, and the cause of death involves violence, as in PJ's case with the suicide by gunshot, the depth of despair is understandably magnified and traumatic. Bereavement expert Dr. William Worden identified seven "mediators of mourning,"[10] or factors that influence the survivor's response to a death. Many of these were reflected in PJ's case—for example, PJ's age and gender, the deceased person's relationship to her, the nature of the attachment, the mode of death, prior losses, and family grief. PJ lost her father at a critical point in her own development and had always been seeking his approval. She was acutely aware that he was her only remaining parent, in a family that had not adequately mourned her mother's death fourteen years earlier. Since PJ was the youngest of her siblings, still dependent for support through college, her sense of security was destroyed.

THE LONG-TERM IMPACT OF SUICIDE

PJ acknowledged that the long-term effect of her experiences has had a potent impact on her life choices. Noting that she's "had a fairly decent life," PJ said that her husband, whom she married when she was thirty-four but originally met when she was thirteen, also grew up in her hometown. Because her husband "felt 'safe'" to her, PJ had, in effect, "married someone from my past, longing for a past that never was."

After earning her master's degree, PJ has worked at the same state human services job for more than twenty years. During that time, she felt she had "accomplished some good things." She and her husband now have a son and share a "lovely" suburban home. Thanks to her empathy and sense of humor, everyone feels comfortable with PJ, and her experience has allowed her to relate to all kinds of people, since she said she can "connect to their sorrow and pain, the struggle in their lives."

Despite the positive aspects of her life, PJ observed that she was "always looking for security" and didn't "like change or taking risks." Although her father had considerable professional success, PJ told me she preferred not to "stress" herself or be "too ambitious," saying that "for me, success is connected with death." When her husband mentioned wanting to plan for retirement, PJ started thinking, "Is the future going to happen? Is anything safe? Is the world safe? That's my worldview."

As she approached her fiftieth birthday, PJ realized that the underlying question she constantly asked herself was, "Is it safe?" She reasoned that "if I don't take risks, nothing bad will happen." She began "getting freaked out" by the thought that within a year, she would have outlived both her mother and her sister Carrie, who had died at the age of forty-nine, and was "close to outliving [her] father." She pondered a string of odd coincidences involving significant dates in her life—that her sister had died exactly forty-three years after the date of her mother's death, that her son was born exactly ten years after the date of her father's death, that her husband and her mother shared the same birthday, and that she and her husband's mother shared a birthday— finding these "cosmic threads of connection within [her] family . . . very comforting."

RESOLUTION

As her older sister Carrie neared death, PJ had two insights that reflected her healing and growth. Cognizant of how devastating the long-term psychological effects of her earlier losses had been, PJ was determined to "do this death thing correctly." Because Carrie had been ill with colon cancer for two and a half years before she died, she and PJ had many conversations and were able to process Carrie's wishes and the prospect of her death during that time.

PJ described her sister as "so brave [and] so positive." When this latest death occurred, PJ said, she was "an adult" and "in control of [her] mourning." And since PJ "was not dependent on" Carrie, her "emotions were much purer." She was able to mourn her sister "deeply" and found the experience "very different from the death of my parents."

Survivors such as PJ, and the two women in Washington, D.C., whose stories introduced this section, appreciate the length of time that lingering illnesses such as cancer provide for grieving. PJ realized that this type of death gives survivors more time to process their relationship with their loved one, to review their lives together, to provide support, and to discuss the dying person's often-unspoken feelings about how he or she wishes to die. This "anticipatory grieving" allowed PJ to mourn the past she and Carrie had shared, her sister's current state of decline, what PJ was losing in the moment, and finally the loss of a shared future with each other and with their families.

THE DYING PROCESS INFLUENCES GRIEVING

Research has shown that *how* survivors experience the dying process with their loved ones has a profound effect on their grief after their loved one dies. If the dying process is very lengthy, the predeath experience can become unhealthy. Much as you love the person who is dying, providing care for him or her can put a real strain on personal energy and other family, social, occupational, and financial obligations. This may result in "caregiver distress," a condition that interferes with your capacity for prolonged caretaking and often causes burnout. If your caregiving duties produce "compassion fatigue," you may experience feelings of guilt and resentment that could inhibit a healthy grieving process after your loved one is gone and lead to complicated grief. In cases such as this, you may benefit from professional help.

On the other hand, if the process is healthy, as it was in PJ's experience with her sister's death, bereavement may be less painful and more resolved, enabling survivors to move on and reinvest in life more fully.

ADVANTAGES OF BEING A NORMALIZER

The outstanding advantage of normalizers is that *they know who they are and what they want from life*. Their values, priorities, and interests emanate from their desire for "normalcy," however they define this. They make conscious choices to find or create a role in life that provides them with security. They are committed to their family and community, often playing an active role in events and activities involving their children and family. They are concerned about quality of life, particularly as it affects their immediate circle. They tend to be contributors to their community, church, neighborhood, or the social causes they embrace. Examples we saw include a husband and father who established his family in a community near where his father's death had disrupted his own childhood, and a couple who created a new family by adoption after the tragic deaths of their son and daughter.

Another advantage was pointed out to me by a wonderful woman I had the privilege of counseling several years after her husband of more than forty years had died. She observed that many older widows actively opted for "living to the fullest" because of their heightened sense of mortality following the loss of their long-term companions. They determined to maintain a lifestyle similar to the one they had shared with their husbands, but without remarrying. Some chose to enjoy their new identity as single women, without the obligations or burdens of their former life. They would continue to "travel, dance, and have fun," with or without a companion, and "live in the now." She suggested that for some, this is how they stayed connected to their loved one, even as they made a new beginning.

She observed that others chose to revert to who they used to be—"before the compromises of marriage and togetherness." In chapter 1, I quoted Dr. Therese Rando as saying that "your identity changes as you slowly make the change from a 'we' to an 'I.'"[11] The widow I counseled observed that going from a "we" to an "I" can be a positive identity shift: "You can resort to the 'before' personality, which was lost during the marriage."

Being a normalizer, then, offers some interesting possibilities.

DISADVANTAGES OF BEING A NORMALIZER

In their zeal to achieve normalcy, normalizers may make certain kinds of mistakes. They may avoid experiencing the painful feelings of loss, a necessary component of the grieving process. They may miss opportunities to explore new options for living their changed lives. Concerned about suffering additional losses or becoming stuck in an unhappy situation, they may refuse (both consciously and unconsciously) to make commitments to new relationships, to a stable lifestyle with a home and steady work. They may become inflexible and avoid taking risks, such as exploring a new career or moving to a new place, that offer potential advantages. Conversely, they can make hasty decisions— changing a job, selling a house, or getting involved with a new partner—before adequately thinking them through. They may lock themselves into what feels familiar and safe in order to provide comfort and fill the void left by their absent loved one, only to find that they later regret their decision.

In certain cases, survivors and other victims of trauma repress their unbearable memories in order to function. These normalizers overcompensate for their loss by denying its life-altering effect on them. They soldier on with their lives in "stiff-upper-lip" style, doing what needs to be done to survive, avoiding any reflection on their experience and the feelings it evokes. This has occurred with some family members who lost loved ones in the September 11 attacks as well as the Holocaust.

Judith Guest's 1976 novel *Ordinary People* offers a powerful example of the potential disadvantages of the normalizer approach to dealing with death. As we saw in chapter 2 the story focuses on a successful couple, Calvin and Beth, and their two sons, Buck and Conrad. In the aftermath of a boating accident in which Buck, the older son, drowns while Conrad survives, the remaining members of the family exhibit strikingly different styles of coping with the tragedy. Conrad displays the nomad's typical inability to handle death. Profoundly grief-stricken, he attempts suicide and is hospitalized. After his discharge from the hospital, Conrad enters treatment with a psychiatrist, who eventually helps him come to terms with Buck's death and begin to heal. Meanwhile, Calvin struggles with his surviving son's problems while grieving Buck's death. Both Conrad and Calvin have trouble understanding Beth's single-minded determination to "get back to normal."[12] Her inability to grieve with her husband and son, communicate her feelings, and comfort her surviving son results in her leaving her family. Beth's denial creates an irreparable rift in their understanding of one another.

Normalizers need to learn to take *appropriate risks* for the future. Since their tendency is to create or re-create the patterns of relationship and lifestyle they lost, they should try not to fall into old patterns. They should avoid allowing their life to become too narrow and limiting, as many of these stories show. For example, normalizers who have repressed the past must exhume it in order to come to terms with the profound loss they want to forget. Exploring their grief may be a huge risk for these normalizers. Conversely, normalizers who emulated the past must examine whether doing so is truly consistent with who they want to become in their postloss life.

STRATEGIES FOR HEALING AND GROWTH

Like other grievers, normalizers will need to seek support and help from various sources. Initially, they may find comfort with close friends and family. Because they value being part of the community, normalizers often seek help through their church or synagogue or through bereavement support groups composed of people who have shared similar experiences. Widow-to-widow groups are examples.

However, within a period of time—a year, perhaps two

years, depending on the individual—their need for this kind of support may shift. Being alone or "out of the mainstream" of our social structure may stimulate a desire for new companions to share weekly pastimes, such as going to the movies or out to dinner, or perhaps more extensive activities such as travel. Eventually, normalizers seek the security of another relationship or another family, in an attempt to regain what they lost in order to feel fulfilled.

To identify potential sources of support and assistance, ask yourself the following questions:

- Whom could I seek out for comfort?
- What resources are available to me? Friends? Family? Community?
- What resources or supporters could point me toward other resources?

Evaluate what you did and didn't enjoy about the relationship you lost. Which aspects of your life and relationship do you want to keep? Which would you like to change?

Normalizers would do well to consult with a professional grief counselor before making any major decisions, such as selling their house, changing jobs, or dating seriously. Forming their new identity as normalizers must involve making sure that their new life is their *conscious choice* rather than an attempt to replicate their former life merely because they were comfortable with it. For instance, I've encountered many stories of "rebound marriages" that failed because the surviving spouses made impulsive decisions to marry someone they thought was just like their deceased spouse. Idealizing a deceased spouse without sufficient time or consideration can lead to mistakes that may be emotionally, physically, and financially draining.

As you consider the key decisions facing you, ponder these issues:

- What did you enjoy most about your relationship with your loved one?
- What did you enjoy least about that relationship?
- What is a priority for you to re-create in your life?
- Which decisions can you hold off on until some time has passed?
- With whom could you consult before making big decisions?
- Who do you want to be now?

QUESTIONS FOR FURTHER EXPLORATION

Are you most like the normalizer?

1. Have you tried to create the life you wanted but didn't have because of your loss? Or, have you tried to re-create the kind of life you had before your loss, and want to have again? List the specific ways you've tried, and the decisions you've made to have a normalizer's life.
2. Do you avoid experiencing painful feelings of loss? Do you avoid taking risks or are you inflexible in any way? Do you ever make hasty decisions without adequately thinking through how and if you will benefit from the outcome of the decision?
3. Are there ways you've reacted to your loss that aren't beneficial to you? If so, how and why? What decisions should you make in your life to help you heal?

4. How do you understand the relationship between the loss you experienced and the way you live your life now? Are you comfortable with the normalizer identity?

REFLECTIONS FOR THE NORMALIZER

Reacting to profound losses in your life by actively and creatively pursuing the life you want is an attempt to remake your world into the place you want it to be. There are many benefits to doing this. You are connected to life and your community. You want to make a difference in your community and feel that the way you live your life matters.

Asking yourself the questions above may help you identify all the ways you've reacted to your loss, unconsciously and consciously, and how you will live your life going forward. Evaluate the decisions you have made. Are there ways that you think your growth has been limited or inhibited by your reactions to this experience? Perhaps you are so committed to your vision of a life re-created after loss that you haven't been willing or able to take risks that would benefit you. I ask you to consider these difficult questions because there may be ways you can live an even happier, more productive, and meaningful life after your loss.

Five

The Activist

To know and not to act is not to know.
—Yukio Mishima, *The Sea of Fertility*

WHO ARE THE ACTIVISTS? The men and women who choose the activist path in response to their losses feel a sense of social justice, compassion, and empathy for others. They manifest these beliefs and emotions by choosing roles in life that make a contribution to others' quality of life. About 20 percent of those I interviewed were activists. They want to make a difference in the world. They use their talents and passion as social activists, writers and artists, business leaders, scientists, and politicians. More than the other identities, activists possess a drive and a dedication that turn the experience of loss into a catalyst for influencing positive change. Activists exhibit an *outward* and *future* orientation and are highly conscious of the value of time. They often have a heightened sense of their own mortality and therefore feel pressured by the limits of their time on earth to accomplish goals that benefit others.

The definition of the activist identity can be summed up in the words of Bertolt Brecht: "Do not fear death so much, but rather the inadequate life."[1]

THE TYPICAL ACTIVIST

After John Walsh's six-year-old son Adam was abducted and murdered in 1981, Walsh transmuted his grief into leadership and activism. One of his efforts, *America's Most Wanted*, has been one of the most watched programs on television since 1988. Dedicated to finding criminals and sexual predators and bringing them to justice, host Walsh and his audience have contributed to the FBI's capture of more than one thousand fugitives. Beyond Walsh's commitment to justice, however, was the personal tragedy that motivated him.

> The Walsh family's tragic story woke up a nation to the danger of child predators after NBC aired two movies about their life. "Adam," in 1983 and "Adam: His Song Continues" in 1986, dramatized the incredible heartbreak and then resilience of the Walshes. . . .
>
> [Their] experience taught them that the nation was in desperate need of leadership in the fight to protect children, and they decided to create something positive out of their personal tragedy.[2]

The Walshes' efforts have led to an array of invaluable resources. These include the National Center for Missing and Exploited Children (NCMEC) and the hotline 1-800-THE-LOST, not only for parents and children but also for law enforcement in the United States and internationally. Walsh has effectively used a variety of media—books, DVDs, the Internet (www.missingkids.com), as well as television—to educate the public about child predators. Finally, exactly twenty-five years after Adam's death, John and Revè Walsh were present in the White House Rose Garden in 2006 to watch President George W. Bush sign the Adam Walsh Child Protection and Safety Act, to track sex offenders after their release from prison.

Adam's death transformed John Walsh into an activist. With the unyielding support of his wife, Revè, Walsh abandoned a lucrative real estate development career to become a committed social activist, championing the protection of our country's most vulnerable citizens—our children.

Activism and Altruism

Browsing through a Borders bookstore one day in June 2003, I noticed the cover of *Psychology Today,* and was drawn to the lead story, "The Making of an Activist."[3] Some psychologists suggest that there are a number of reasons why people become activists, including parental modeling, personality, interest in public issues, and timing. For example, growing up in the 1960s and being inspired by leaders such as Bobby Kennedy and Martin Luther King Jr raised the social consciousness of millions of baby boomers. I would add to this explanation that for survivors of loss, there are two further reasons: (1) sharing a collective identity with others who have also experienced the death of a loved one, and (2) developing a sense of altruism.

Some researchers see altruism, defined as devotion to the interest of others, as a desire to help oneself. Debra Mashek, PhD, a research fellow studying moral emotions at George Mason University, explains that "having a sense of collective identity means that the world is my community, therefore, I am also helping myself."[4] Professor Jeffrey Kottler of California State University calls altruism "reciprocal. The more you can get out of yourself and reach out to others, the more meaningful and satisfying life can be."[5]

PROFILES OF ACTIVISTS

Activists use their personal experience of loss and their appreciation for their own mortality to make a difference. Suffering exists in countless ways in the world. Activists are dedicated to helping others who have also lost loved ones, whether suddenly or through long and painful illnesses. This identity reflects their new mission in life.

Eileen: Helping Others through Social Justice

Eileen is a prominent leader in a major city whose public persona belies the emotional pain she suffered as the result of a loss in early childhood. Her need to contribute exemplifies the activist. People with this identity type understand human suffering, loss, and the toll they take on the human spirit and are compelled to act on behalf of others. As a result, Eileen has devoted herself to improving the quality of life, interracial relations, and social welfare in places as diverse as Boston, Massachusetts, and Ukraine.

To explain how her loss influenced her, Eileen started by describing the sudden death of her father from a heart attack at the age of thirty-six, which left her mother to raise seven-year-old Eileen, her nine-year-old sister, and her ten-month-old brother. Eileen told me that "the reality of [her] father's death sank in" only when her mother took a job. Failing to gain attention and recognition from her mother, Eileen "focused on achieving success." Ten years of what Eileen termed "fairly normal family life" passed, after which Eileen's mother "fell apart" following her brother's Bar Mitzvah and was hospitalized for the first time.

Eileen's quest for recognition started with earning a dollar from her grandfather as a reward for good grades. As she grew older, she progressed to becoming actively involved with B'nai Brith, "a Jewish organization that cultivated young leaders" saying that the group "fulfilled many of my needs for recognition. I developed a strong commitment to their activities and the successes they brought me."

It occurred to Eileen that her family's experience "could happen to anyone," and she realized how fortunate they were to have had grandparents who lived in the same house and uncles who were able to provide financial help. But, she noted, "Not everyone has a support system." Eileen wondered how other people who suffered similar losses managed to get along, thinking, "There but for the grace of God go I." Eileen's experience of early loss led her to develop a "passion for fairness and justice" and to make social justice "the focus of [her] work throughout [her] career."

"The impact of my father's death on *who I am today*," Eileen said, "has been overwhelming." She characterized his death as having left "a hole" in her life—a hole that she fills through her career in social work and activism in the Jewish community, which she "care[s] deeply about." She observed that, for her, "the only way to feel good on the inside is by doing good on the outside." Her faith-based work gives Eileen what she called "a warm sense of community and a strong network of friends [that she] didn't have in [her] family structure." She summed up her activist orientation like this: "I feel good about it. I have meaning in my life, and I will not go to my grave feeling I didn't do what I wanted to do."

Donna: How a Grandfather with Alzheimer's Changed Her Purpose in Life

This book is about the long-term impact of the *death* of a loved one on survivors. For many family members, however, the loss of a loved one due to Alzheimer's disease is regarded as a "living death," because you lose the relationship you had with the person you knew and loved. Your loved one can no longer remember how to do the daily activities we all take for granted, such as dressing, bathing, cooking, and managing money. Your uncle remains alive in body only; his memory and mental abilities have faded away. Your grandmother may begin to forget where she is. She loses her sense of time. Eventually, she no longer recognizes you.

Donna's grandfather Pepe lived with Donna and her parents for several years after his wife's death. Hearing Pepe's stories of his experiences as the owner of a general store as well as "a gardener, a craftsman, a landlord, a father, and a grandfather," Donna came to appreciate "what a full life" he'd lived. But as Pepe's Alzheimer's progressed, he eventually began having memory problems and mood swings and became "difficult to manage." They first moved him into an assisted-living facility, then into a nursing home, where he remained bedridden. By this point, Pepe would introduce Donna as his grandson or perhaps his nephew, or ask, "Who are you again?"

When her grandfather finally died at the age of ninety-two, after what Donna termed "a rapid progression of the disease," she felt a range of emotions—sadness at losing him and anger that his quality of life in the nursing home hadn't been better. Like so many other surviving family members, she also felt guilt because she "was glad it was over." Her experience inspired her to volunteer at a local senior center, where she has learned valuable lessons about herself and life.

Donna said that caring for her grandfather made her aware "that anything can happen at any time" and led her to realize that she wanted to spend more time with her parents, who are in their sixties. Although her professional background was in a mortgage company, Donna noted that her "priorities and values have changed, too," since her caregiving experience taught her the pleasure of "working with people, being a helper." Donna described herself not only as having become "more patient" but also as having gained an "increased . . . awareness of social attitudes toward old people." Donna came to believe that this country treats the elderly as "disposable" instead of venerating them and celebrating their lives as other societies do.

With this newfound insight, Donna decided to change careers and work with Alzheimer's patients as a professional. She is exploring her options for programs in gerontology at various colleges and looks forward to making her contribution to the quality of life of the elders with whom she works.

Darrell: From Businessman to Social Activist

Darrell Scott's seventeen-year-old daughter Rachel was the first student murdered in the Columbine High School massacre in 1999. When I attended an event at which he spoke, I was moved by his determination to spread his daughter's work and talk about how his daughter's death had changed his life.

In the book *Chain Reaction: Call to Compassionate Revolution*, which Scott wrote with Steve Rabey, Scott honors Rachel by describing this extraordinary young woman's belief in the power of kindness—that every act of kindness sets off a "chain reaction" that benefits others and can change the world. In keeping with her philosophy, Rachel reached out to kids "who were low on the school totem pole," kids who were viewed as outcasts, bullies, and even outsiders such as Eric and Dylan, the young men who ultimately killed her. A typical teenager in many ways, she kept a journal of drawings and writings that revealed her faith in God, her belief that she would have a positive impact on the world, and premonitions that she would die at a young age.

Determined to carry on her legacy, Scott left his high-level corporate position and is devoting his life to stopping youth violence. In addition to writing several books, consulting to politicians and educators, and speaking to more than five million people around the world, he has created a multifaceted educational program for middle school and high school students called "Rachel's Challenge." Personally training student leaders on how to achieve Rachel's message of kindness and compassion, he has delivered these programs to more than a thousand schools in the United States, Canada, Latin America, and elsewhere throughout the world. In addition, Scott has been on all the major TV talk shows, such as *Larry King Live* and *The Oprah Winfrey Show*.

Here's how he sees his role as the carrier of his daughter's message for compassion:

> Although I don't claim to be the world's greatest public speaker or writer, I feel this is what I have been called to do right now. I didn't ask to be connected to one of the thirteen people who would be killed at Columbine, but I am. As a result, part of what I feel I am called to do with my life right now is to speak and write about how all of us can take the experience of Columbine and learn something from it.[6]

THE BENEFITS OF SHARING PERSONAL STORIES

Many authors, like Darrell Scott, have written books not only to share their experience with others but also to help other survivors better understand the impact of loss on their lives. Hope Edelman, a journalist, wrote about the long-term effect of her mother's death on her life in her best-selling book *Motherless Daughters*. Her message touched so many women that she followed it up with a compilation of stories "from daughters who, as many as thirty years after their mothers' deaths, continued to renegotiate their relationships with their mothers and admitted to missing them . . . still."[7] As a result, support groups have sprung up all over the country, offering safe places for women to find comfort with other women who understand their pain. By sharing her story, and by reaching out to the broad community of women who have lost their mothers, she defined a "collective identity" of "motherless daughters." She has found meaning and purpose from her loss and made a positive impact on the lives of so many other women.

Sharing personal stories enables readers not only to learn from other people's experiences but also to take comfort in knowing that they are not alone in their grief and that feeling sadness throughout their lives is a common reaction to the death of a loved one.

Another benefit to reaching out is the opportunity to connect with friends and family members. This was the case when my cousin Rachel phoned urgently one day to alert me to a discussion on a local talk show about Edelman's newly published book, *Motherless Daughters*. Twenty-two years ago, Rachel and I both lost our mothers. Despite having deep attachments to our mothers and sweet affection for our respective aunts, we had not spoken much of our mothers since. Talking about being motherless daughters awakened our memories and allowed Rachel and me to revisit our relationships with our mothers and with each other. The choices we made for our lives after our mothers' deaths reflected the priorities we had developed as a result of losing them. Rachel married her longtime boyfriend the following year with plans to have a family. With a husband and three-year-old daughter, I entered a graduate program in social work in hopes of making a difference in the world.

Amanda: Far-Reaching Ramifications of Long-Ago Decisions

Amanda's story illustrates how the actions of one generation can cascade through several generations and how culture can influence decisions that have long-range effects on families. Amanda and I met in a bereavement class about how to improve our professional skills as caregivers. Both of us were social workers working with elderly people and their families. Amanda is an attractive Chinese-American woman in her early thirties who worked part-time to ensure that she would be home when her two young sons finished nursery school each day. Getting to know Amanda was a pleasure because she was so focused regarding her work with elders and yet just as clear about how her career complemented her family life. Upon hearing about my book, she offered to tell me her story.

Amanda explained that her parents had entered into an arranged marriage in Hong Kong in the late 1950s, when her mother was fifteen and her father twenty-five. Since her mother's family was poor, her maternal grandparents had sought a wealthy husband for her, in hopes of providing not just for her mother but for her mother's family as well. "There wasn't any chemistry" between her parents, observed Amanda, "but they liked each other so they were married."

AMANDA'S FATHER'S LEGACY

Like many young men his age, this new husband had his own agenda: to start from scratch in America rather than live off his family's wealth. With the help of his sister, Amanda's father arrived in Boston, Massachusetts, speaking fluent English, with a college degree, a young wife, and great hopes of becoming a businessman. He could find work, however, only as a bartender in a Chinese restaurant, working 3:00 P.M. to 2:00 A.M. six days a week and earning a limited income even with tips. Amanda's father decided he wanted a family, a boy, "badly," because, as Amanda explained, "In our culture, boys are more valued to carry on the family name than girls. Six years after my sister and I were born, my father's wish for a son was granted."

During the first nine years of Amanda's life, the family struggled along. Her happiest memories, she recalled, were of her father's day off—"terrific Tuesdays"—when he spent time with her at the park. Her mother, on the other hand, was overwhelmed by the demands of motherhood. While her husband worked, Amanda's mother went out, leaving her children at home alone. Resentful over losing her own childhood and being pushed into marriage with a man she did not love, her mother acted like a teenager, wanting to have fun. She would say to Amanda, "Big sister, give me something to eat." Amanda explained that after school, the children were left at home by themselves with no one to bathe or care for them. Having no cooking skills and no idea how to feed her baby brother, Amanda mostly "stayed by the window looking for her [mother's] car." She was "too scared" to sleep, feeling that she "had to take care of them." This continued "for two to three years."

When her father was admitted to the hospital at age forty-two, he was diagnosed with cancer of the liver, a disease that the doctor informed him was common among Asian men born and raised in China, due to sanitation problems involving the water and food. Her mother became protective of her children, not letting them visit him in the hospital. For his part, Amanda's father didn't want his children to be scared and remember him that way. Her father did manage to come home "for a couple of nights" for Chinese New Year, but Amanda remembers him then as "very thin, a changed man," with "sunken cheeks." She described herself as "horrified, terrified; he looked like the starving people with bloated bellies." After an ambulance took her father back to the hospital, "No one in the family said anything."

THE EMOTIONAL IMPACT OF HER FATHER'S DEATH

When Amanda awoke the next day, the house felt different. She saw her mother and grandmother cooking, black clothes laid out for her, with black stickers on her red slippers—she explained that wearing red is disrespectful to the dead, so the slippers had to be covered with black. Amanda's mother told her, "Daddy died. He fell asleep and is never going to wake up." Amanda says her first thought was, "I'll never go to sleep again!" When Amanda attended the funeral, she found herself overwhelmed by "all the plants and the smell of the flowers." After the funeral, the family spent a week in a hotel while her mother returned home to cook in order "to leave food for the spirit of [her] father, who was supposed to return for a feast." Since the family had to dress in black for a month, Amanda "dreaded going to school," saying, "The kids made fun of me." In the aftermath of her father's death, Amanda said, "There was no safe, happy place for me to be."

In describing the "residual effect" of her father's death on her even now, Amanda mentioned her fear of funeral homes and hospitals and her aversion to having plants and flowers around, since she associated them with the funeral home. "I became an introvert to avoid others," she observed, "because I felt alienated, neglected, or abandoned by everybody."

But her father's legacy wasn't entirely negative. Amanda noted that the man she married is "gentle like [her] father," that he "is [her] soul mate," and that they "have two wonderful boys." In short, she says, "I value every moment I have on earth."

Amanda's Priorities and Values

Amanda's beliefs, values, and priorities were shaped by her early childhood experiences as well as her Chinese culture, which places a high value on excelling in school. Choosing her profession was an expression of her values. Determined to help people, Amanda worked her way through Boston University with a "skyrocketing GPA," earning both her undergraduate degree and a master's in social work. Because she didn't "want anyone to go through what [she] went through as a child," she demonstrated great courage and found her calling by facing her fears and opting for an internship in a hospital intensive care unit. Amanda explained that at first, she "felt terrified" and "had flashbacks to [her] father." But as she began to work as part of a team with other medical professionals, saw "patients progressing," and helped set up community services, she realized that she "loved hospitals" and discovered that "as a social worker, I can prevent others from being hurt." Although she eventually "decided that working with children brought back too many memories" for her, Amanda found working with the elderly to be enjoyable and rewarding. In her words: "I am making a difference in other people's lives."

Resolution

After Amanda's first son was born, she and her mother became close. She began to empathize with her mother, as she began to experience all the responsibilities of motherhood.

Through therapy and through her study of loss and bereavement, Amanda reflected on her mother's life experiences and came to realize that her grandmother had essentially "pushed her [mother] out in her teens." Amanda said that having children of her own made her "very responsive to others" and gave her a much deeper understanding of her mother.

When her mother dismissed Amanda's memories with "It was a long time ago," Amanda replied, "I have forgiven you, but I haven't forgotten. I am OK." She added, "These experiences have made me stronger, the person I am today." Amanda's profound insight is a powerful expression of how she has healed. Psychologist Claudia Black sums it up like this: "Forgiving is not forgetting. It is remembering and letting go."[8]

Forgiveness

What is forgiveness, and why is it important? According to Dr. Aaron Lazare, professor of psychiatry at the University of Massachusetts Medical School, forgiveness is "the emotional and cognitive process by which the offended party or victim relinquishes grudges, feelings of hatred, bitterness, animosity, or resentment toward the offender."[9]

In his book *On Apology*, Lazare discusses the complex relationship between forgiveness and apology. Forgiveness, he adds, represents a change of mind and heart from the victim to the wrongdoer, suggesting that forgiveness goes beyond apology. Neither is easy, but he explains that apology is necessary for forgiveness to occur.

South African theologian and 1984 Nobel Peace Prize winner Bishop Desmond Tutu believes that "to forgive is not just to be altruistic. It is the best form of self-interest. What dehumanizes you inexorably dehumanizes me. [Forgiveness] gives people resilience, enabling them to survive and emerge still human despite all efforts to dehumanize them." Speaking to a BBC reporter in 2005 about the tenth anniversary of South Africa's democracy, and how the country was "turned around," Tutu, who chaired the Truth and Reconciliation Commission, explained: Nelson Mandela's "spectacular" example of forgiveness and reconciliation was a model for the country. He went on to say that "our people realized that when you harbor anger and resentment, and even when you carry out acts of revenge, those are things that actually destroy you."[10]

Ann: Becoming a Grief Counselor

Ann's story exemplifies the evolution from mother-teacher to "activist–grief counselor" as a result of her ten-year-old daughter's sudden death seven years earlier from viral myocarditis. When her daughter came home from school complaining of a sore tummy, Ann told me she thought it must be chicken pox, since her son had it at the time. But when her condition worsened, they took her to the hospital, and "within thirty-six hours, she was gone."

Ann found it "a bit challenging" to plan a mourning period that would mix the family's Irish culture with American rituals. She said that Irish tradition involved "lay[ing] the child in the bed and spend[ing] time with the body until the burial, which takes place within three days. Especially for children, we have a vigil to protect them." Observing that Americans "are more uncomfortable with death," Ann told me her family decided to have "an open-casket wake at the funeral home." Here's how she described the somewhat unexpected results:

Some adults were blown away, but the children came around the casket, they hung around her [daughter], checked on her. Some of them touched her to feel that she was cold. Because the kids were comfortable, the adults became more comfortable, too.

Since Ann's daughter died in early spring, when it was too cold for a burial, the family had her cremated, which, as Ann put it, "means mobility," since now her daughter "can always come with us."

Although the whole family was "in shock," Ann said her eight- and eleven-year-old sons "had trouble expressing their feelings" and her husband "refused to talk about it." Since the boys were active in sports, Ann "thought they should continue with their normal activities" for the time being. She decided the wisest course of action would be for her "to take care of [herself in order] to be prepared when [her] children were ready to grieve." Attending a parents' group proved very helpful because it allowed Ann to share her grief with parents who had suffered similar losses. After several months, Ann brought her children to the local Center for Grieving Children, which not only collected sympathy cards from Ann's daughter's classmates but also gave the family "memory books" at the end of the year. According to Ann, the books told "little stories about her that [Ann] didn't know" and "were lovely for [her] to read," since, in Ann's words, "Kids can really tap into what loss is about."

Ann described the death of her only daughter as having affected her life "really intensely," in part because Ann's "only prior experience with death" was grieving for her parents. Ann said she "felt a huge feminine connection," but, "since I had no mother, this connection was lost when [our daughter] left us." Due to what Ann termed "the strain of our daughter's death," coupled with "the lack of communication between us," Ann and her husband grew apart and divorced within a few years.

Two years after her daughter's death, Ann began volunteering at the Center for Grieving Children. Describing herself as "hungry for knowledge," Ann said she "wanted to learn more about how we as human beings navigate this journey of life together." She eventually completed the center's training program, because, as she put it, "I wanted to give back." Ann joined the center's staff as its community outreach director. She summed up her activism by saying, "I feel passionate about this work. So many children are grieving, it's very scary. Who's taking care of them?"

After a national search by the Center for Grieving Children's board of directors in 2001, Ann was selected to be the center's executive director, being perfectly suited to the challenge of guiding the center "toward fulfilling its vision of serving as the beacon of light in the hearts and souls of grieving children throughout the world."[11]

Barry: Leadership in the Wake of Multiple Losses

A final example of an activist illustrates how one loss can cascade into multiple losses, such as the place we work, our job, and the environment in which we live. These losses challenge our long-held beliefs about who we are and why we are here on earth.

Barry was a dedicated public servant who had worked for the City of New York for thirty-three years. As director of operations for the New York City Port Authority tunnels, terminals, and bridges, he oversaw eleven hundred civilians and three hundred police officers. His office in the World Trade Center contained many personal effects—awards, photos of his family and his beloved dog. He described it as "my second home from 1971."

During the September 11, 2001, attacks, Barry lost sixteen employees and a number of good friends. There were close calls in his family as well. His son-in-law was able to escape from the World Trade Center building where he worked, and the day before, Barry's sister had been on the same flight that crashed into Barry's building. In the following year, Barry attended numerous funerals, speaking at many of them. Witnessing the mourning and grief of so many families took a toll on him physically, emotionally, and spiritually. He gained considerable weight, experienced anxiety from the responsibility of "keeping things going," and endured a crisis of faith over how God could allow so much anguish and tragedy.

Looking back on his ordeal several years later, Barry reflected that "the grieving process is lifelong; it scars you." Recalling the "spectacular" view of the Twin Towers that he once had on his daily drive to New York from New Jersey, Barry described how he used to start crying whenever he looked up at the absence of the towers. When Barry's staff gave him a Star of David crafted from World Trade Center steel, he realized that seeing that steel every day had "made no impact on me" but that "this star, this new symbol, makes me cry because I have lost it. I don't look up anymore."

In the aftermath of the attacks, when Barry was "dealing with the crisis and trying to keep the agency going," he asked his rabbi, "How can I stay strong?" Answered the rabbi: "Leaders cry." His rabbi not only gave Barry permission to cry but also helped him understand why he had survived. According to Barry, "It's a leadership issue. I know that I made a difference. That's why you're a leader and why I was here. That was my purpose."

Activists: Helping Others Grieve and Heal

In addition to those profiled in this section, the people I interviewed included a seventy-three-year-old woman whose husband had died suddenly thirty-five years earlier, leaving her with four children to raise; a man whose mother had died of cancer when he was fourteen; and an incredibly resilient woman who had experienced multiple losses: her two-year-old son to meningitis, her husband in a car crash six months later, and her infant son to a rare genetic disorder six months after that. All these people have transformed their lives after losing a loved one. Some, like me, have become social workers, psychotherapists, psychologists, and academic researchers. Many others have become grief counselors. All have become activists, dedicated to helping people, individually and collectively. All have become passionate about a cause—and about making a difference.

ADVANTAGES OF BEING AN ACTIVIST

Activists demonstrate tremendous adaptability in the face of loss. They not only understand the inevitability of change, they embrace it. Activists advocate for improvement in the quality of life—through political rights and empowerment, public service and social causes like health care—whether it's on a day-to-day basis in people's hearts and minds or by creating new laws and policies for the next twenty or one hundred years. They are proactive, accomplished, productive, and effective in their sphere of influence—social and public welfare, the environment, the arts, or science. Their goal is to improve the way we think, behave, interact, and ultimately live. They are seen as powerful, able to attract others to their ideas, causes, and actions. They are highly attuned to the world around them, focusing on new trends and new ways of thinking and living. They are extremely energetic; they are innovators.

Activists create positive change. They turn their own loss experience into a mirror of other people's suffering. Sometimes, their loss actually becomes the catalyst for change. I found countless examples: One woman who lost her mother in her teens became a feminist activist. Two young widows whose husbands died on September 11 in hijacked planes have established Beyond the 11th, a nonprofit organization to help widows in Afghanistan affected by war, terrorism, and oppression.[12] A mother whose son died at the World Trade Center during the September 11 attacks has been helping other families maneuver through the bureaucratic requirements to obtain state and federal benefits offered to them after the tragedy.

DISADVANTAGES OF BEING AN ACTIVIST

The sense of being "driven" by a fear of being out of control can wreak havoc on the lives of activists. The void left by the lost loved one must be filled, and activists see themselves as the ones who are required to fill it. Sometimes this "mandate" manifests itself as insatiability or an attempt to meet unrealistic goals. This can cause activists to feel constant dissatisfaction with their life, their work, and their family.

This tendency can lead to chronic anxiety or depression. As a result, activists may be inclined toward self-destructive behaviors. For example, being continually spurred on to achieve, the activist personality doesn't always know how or when to stop and "smell the roses." Their dedicated mission to contribute may therefore compel activists to risk too much—such as damaging their health or losing their families for the sake of a career, financial gain, or devotion to their chosen cause. Ironically, the consequences of their drive may have a negative effect on their family and friends. While the activists' overt goals for helping others may be accomplished on a grand scale, those closest to them may suffer. And when this pattern appears, it may set off a negative cycle that repeats itself over time and through subsequent generations.

STRATEGIES FOR HEALING AND GROWTH

The key strategy for activists is *finding balance*. Driven to make an impact on the world around them, activists are oriented primarily toward the future and have an *outward* perspective. They must learn to turn *inward*, live in the moment, deal with the present, and take care of themselves and those close to them. They must learn to pace themselves, to set limits based on priorities for time, energy, and satisfaction. In the simplest sense, this means allocating time, sacred time, just for themselves—to take a walk, read a book, or write a letter to a close friend. Finding balance among the demands of work, family, and life is the major goal. Activists need to learn to be intimate with themselves and nurture themselves, both physically and psychologically. Taking care of their body through positive health practices—exercise, nutrition, rest, and meditation—can help activists find their center.

Activists must confront issues related to their sense of control of their environment. Because they are often so influential, they may have avoided exploring their own vulnerabilities. They need to awaken their spiritual aspect, give up their need to control everything in their lives, and acknowledge and practice "surrender." Activists would be wise to cultivate *inner awareness* and *peace* so that they can validate themselves and the meaning of their postloss lives.

Having read the stories of other activists, you may have determined that you are an activist. Since activists are prone to rapid-fire decision making and action, it would be beneficial to examine more fully your own story, to reflect on the impact the loss of your loved one has had on your life and identity, and how you have transformed your purpose in life.

QUESTIONS FOR FURTHER EXPLORATION

Are you most like the activist?

1. What lessons from your loss experience have motivated you to become an activist?
2. How have you turned your loss into activism? List all the things that you have done that you consider activist responses to your loss. For example, how have you become involved in your cause or community to make a difference in the world?
3. What have you done to make the world a better place and improve the quality of life for others?
4. After experiencing your loss, what is your mission in life now? Why? How have you let others know about your renewed purpose?
5. Are there ways your activities don't benefit you and your family? Do you think you have balance in your

life? Are you able to be an activist and still be there for those close to you? How do your activities distract you from your own needs?

6. How do you understand the relationship between the loss you experienced and the way you live your life now? Are you comfortable with the activist identity?

REFLECTIONS FOR THE ACTIVIST

There is a big difference between writing a check for a cause you support and agreeing to serve on the board of that organization. As an activist, you want to be directly involved.

Transforming the loss you experienced into positive energy that changes the world and makes it a better place is admirable. There are many benefits to being an activist. You demonstrate your adaptability in the face of loss, you embrace change, and you advocate improvements in the quality of life for many.

You are mission driven, and your mission most likely involves helping others. There are ways, however, that your activities may have downsides and may result in distracted neglect. Because activists are so involved in their mission, they may lose a sense of balance and perspective. By not living in the moment, activists may avoid their own painful feelings or the needs of those closest to them. By asking yourself the questions above, perhaps you can identify the ways you have been neglecting your needs and the needs of your loved ones in order to serve those outside of your inner circle. Are there ways you can continue to be an activist yet still be aware of your needs and take care of yourself and your loved ones?

Six
———

The Seeker

The spiritual dimension cannot be ignored, for it is
what makes us human.
—Viktor Frankl, psychiatrist and Holocaust survivor,
from *The Doctor and the Soul*

WHO ARE THE SEEKERS? Seekers experience the death of
a loved one as a catalyst for exploring the spiritual questions
about life. Their loss may stimulate inquiry into the meaning
of life and the reasons why they are here. When a life that
had definition, purpose, and attachments disappears, either
suddenly or through a gradual dying process, those left behind
are likely to ask difficult questions: Why am I here? Where
did I come from? Where is the one who died going? Will we
meet again? What can I do with my life now?

For seekers, life and death become a search for understanding of ourselves and our relationship to the universe.
Seekers actively pursue knowledge from classical philosophy, Eastern and Western religions, or ancient wisdom of
indigenous cultures throughout the world. Their focus is on
exploring the spiritual, the sacred, and the divine. Some

are looking for approaches to attain a higher level of consciousness, a transcendence of this reality, and others want to harness cosmic energy for the higher purpose of helping all human beings here on earth or to understand the connections among all living things. By doing so, seekers are making meaning from their loss.

Seekers live in the present because they believe that the present moment is the only "truth" we can really know. They accept that humans are mortal, and they tend to understand that everything in life changes. Grief heightens their awareness. Yet they also value the mystery of life. They are likely to believe that human beings are more than flesh and blood. They may believe that we have a soul or a spirit that transcends earthly reality. It is *energy*. This belief helps them find meaning in life. It guides them toward fulfilling their potential and their life purpose.

THE TYPICAL SEEKER

My friend Matthew, whom I have known for many years, has spent the past five years living in Chiang Mai, Thailand, and is a practicing Buddhist. He recently wrote to me about his thoughts on how loss has affected people he knew:

> One of the things I have observed throughout the years is the number of people who became famous in Buddhism after a great loss. The great Zen master Dogen, founder of the Soto Zen school, which was the precursor to the San Francisco Zen Center, had both his parents die by the time he was eleven. Nakagawa Soen Roshi, a very important Zen master in the rise of Zen in America, also lost his father as a child. Robert,

who was my current teacher's teacher, didn't lose his parents but was sent away from home at the age of two and experienced great psychological trauma.

I think that one of the reasons Buddhism attracts individuals who have experienced loss is because of the Four Noble Truths. These are the main teachings of the dharma, the wisdom the enlightened Buddha gave to the world in the fifth century B.C. The first two core teachings state that life is difficult, that we must free ourselves of the attachments to things, feelings, beliefs, and people that can obscure the reality: *All things change, and we must accept the impermanence in life.* The third teaching is that there is an end to the suffering we experience in what the Buddha called "nirvana"—inner peace, freedom from attachment, and fulfillment. And the fourth and final "truth" is that there is an Eightfold Path we can follow to reach this sense of peace.

Buddhism offers liberation from this suffering, whatever it may be. The purpose of meditation practice is to bring all those "shadows of forgotten ancestors" into consciousness so they can be acknowledged and finally let go. It is, however, only one option for seekers.

Experiencing the loss of a loved one brings profound sadness and suffering. The grief that people feel can heal, but it takes effort and intention to heal successfully.

This chapter offers stories from seekers who use various spiritual approaches for healing. Some involve formal religions; others are nontraditional by Western standards. As John D. Morgan, director of the King's College Centre for Education about Death and Bereavement in Ontario, explains, "Religion is only one of many aspects of spirituality.

In reflecting on ourselves, we become aware of our limits, and deduce an awareness of the transcendent."[1]

The stories I collected illustrate the many different spiritual paths these seekers chose as a result of their losses. Most were children or teenagers when their loved ones died, but several were adults. Although I would not generalize from these results, I speculate that the loss of a parent in a young person's formative years has a strong impact on his or her psychosocial development. Children and teens are prone to greater self-doubt, self-consciousness about being "different," and may have a harder time answering such questions as Who am I? Where do I fit in the world? Where do I belong?

In addition to pursuing conventional religious beliefs, many seekers find ways for their grief to provide them with opportunities for connection, community, and inner peace. They discover nuances in traditional religions, the practices of ancient cultures, and New Age spirituality.

The Search for Purpose and Meaning

In a recent book, *Awakening to the Sacred*, Lama Surya Das, an American Buddhist leader and teacher, explains why times of sorrow can cause us to search for purpose and meaning in our lives, quoting an old Jewish saying: "God is closest to those with broken hearts." He writes:

> At times of greatest sadness and personal crisis we feel more tenderhearted and closer to our soulful center. When we are most confused and buffeted about by the vagaries of life, we hunger intensely for spiritual guidance and wisdom.
>
> As spiritual seekers, we think about how we can love more deeply, know ourselves more truly, and

connect with the divine more fully. We think about those things that are beyond the self. . . .We think about how we can find ourselves in the whole, the bigger picture, the universal mandala.[2]

Religion and Spirituality

According to theologians, we humans are rational beings, wanting enough order to give coherence and predictability to our lives. Some say that religion helps us understand the ultimate order of the universe and our place in it. It also helps us create order and meaning for our lives. Judaism, Christianity, and Islam believe in a "Creator," called God or Allah, who gives order to the universe and sustains all living things. In contrast, the traditions of indigenous cultures, which live close to their environment, believe in gods, spirits dwelling in nature, and ancestors, all of which contribute to the order of the world. Despite the differences, all religions recognize these beliefs as sacred or holy, connecting us to the larger system of life, which is beyond our immediate understanding.

The death of a loved one challenges our innate desire for order and meaning. It plunges us into emotional and intellectual chaos, the opposite of order. I asked several rabbis and ministers to explain the role of religion and spirituality in helping survivors to heal from their losses.

The Reverend Rosemary Lloyd, associate minister at the First Church of Boston Unitarian Universalist, responded:

Religion is the organized system of theology that binds us together. When a person dies, the church offers opportunities to perform healing rituals, a place to find help and understanding, and a sense of community, where others can bear witness to your loss. It is a place to explore the end to this life and what lives on—both for the person who died and the survivor. The death of any loved one, even a pet, can cause us to ask many questions.

Spirituality is not the same as religion. It is the pursuit of our "higher self" and the values we create to live our daily lives. By developing inner awareness, we become more conscious of our connection to the universe, each other, and the transcendent.

Rabbi Karen Landy, from the liberal Reconstructionist branch of Judaism, teaches rabbinical students and offers spiritual counseling in a large Jewish organization in the Boston area. She explained:

> Religion is a way of organizing our lives. Death and loss challenge us to rejuggle our assumptions about God. After the Holocaust, some groups within Judaism rethought the theology of their old vision of God because if He had been all-powerful, how could the Holocaust have happened? Rather than being omnipotent and able to control all things, God is an *energy force* that connects all of life but isn't all-powerful. God created the world out of chaos, yet chaos remains.

This thinking mirrors that of author Rabbi Harold Kushner, who himself suffered a personal tragedy. His son Aaron was diagnosed with progeria, or "rapid aging," a rare disease that causes stunted height, loss of hair on the head and body, and death in the early teens. Kushner's book *When Bad Things Happen to Good People* has been instrumental in my own grieving process at several different points in my life.

The book is a salve to my sense of injustice about my losses as well as other personal and global tragedies that I believed shouldn't have happened. Kushner writes:

> Is there always a reason, or do some things just happen at random, for no cause? . . .
>
> So it was with God, fashioning a world whose overriding principle was orderliness, predictability, in place of the chaos with which He started. . . . By the end of the sixth day, God had finished the world He had set out to make, and on the seventh day He rested.
>
> But suppose God didn't quite finish by closing time on the afternoon of the sixth day? We know today [from scientists] that the world took billions of years to take shape, not six days. . . . The world is mostly an orderly, predictable place, showing ample evidence of God's thoroughness and handiwork, but pockets of chaos remain.[3]

I have found great comfort in the rabbi's understanding of God as compassionate and powerful yet with limitations as well. If we are cast in God's image, and if the world is constantly evolving, generating the range of all forms—strong and weak, good and evil, harmonious and hostile—can we reasonably expect perfection in all things? Or is it our lifelong challenge to forgive ourselves and our fellow humans for our own limitations?

PROFILES OF SEEKERS

The death of a loved one shapes the seeker by raising questions about what life is about. Someone with this identity searches for answers by focusing on ways to enhance inner awareness and understand their connection to the wider world and the universe. The following stories demonstrate a wide range of religious beliefs and spiritual practices that guide seekers to their own healing.

Miranda: A "Senior Citizen" Orphaned after Her Parents' Deaths

Miranda's ninety-one-year-old father died when she was in her early sixties. Although she described him as having been "a towering figure in my life and not always for good," she "learned forgiveness and compassion" in the last part of his life and even spent two years caring for him when he experienced dementia.

Although Miranda did not adhere to a single spiritual practice, she had explored a variety of traditions, "from Native American spiritualism to Buddhism," and was most impressed by the Dalai Lama's emphasis on compassion and the need for forgiveness. She said her experience of past-life regression taught her that "we will continue to meet those with whom we remain in conflict unless we resolve our issues in the present life." Miranda came to conclude that, in her words, "Life is too short to carry around grudges or 'hurts.' I wanted to be free of this onus."

Describing her father's death as "a transformational experience," Miranda told of spending the last eight days of her father's life at his bedside and feeling both "an enormous sadness at his passing" and "very alone without his presence in my life." She said her feelings of grief and loss "intensified [her] awareness of mortality" and helped her to "become very much at peace with the idea of death." Miranda noted,

"Life also took on a greater meaning, and I became cognizant of [its] brevity. . . . It never ceases to amaze me that in one breath you are alive, and then there is not a next breath! You are gone."

Miranda's sense of aloneness was exacerbated by the fact that she couldn't share her "deep feelings of loss" with her sisters, one of whom found herself unable to forgive their father for what Miranda called "his many missteps during our lives." She even refused to attend his interment. Unlike her sisters, who may suffer unresolved grief in the future, by seeking spiritual guidance to forgive her difficult father, Miranda developed a healthy path to healing, which allowed her to honor him and appreciate their remaining time together.

When her mother died "five years and one month later," Miranda had the satisfaction of realizing that her efforts at organizing her father's financial affairs had allowed Miranda to "secure a good life" for her mother, thereby making her mother's final years very happy.

Following this second parental death, however, Miranda's own sense of loss and aloneness was intensified. Describing the idea of being without parents as "a shock," Miranda became "filled with . . . thoughts of being 'orphaned.'" She expressed the loss of both her parents in stark terms: "It has heightened my sense of being 'on the front line'—that is, my parents' generation is gone, and we are next." Despite Miranda's ongoing "struggle for financial security," she has now become "acutely aware of time" and experiences "a burning desire to enjoy" life.

Miranda's story reminds us that grieving occurs regardless of our own age or the age of our lost loved one. Because ours is a youth-oriented society, we often fail to value our elders, believing that since they have lived a long life, they don't deserve the same level of mourning as others who have died "before their time." In this sense, some bereaved adult children do not receive the same support in their grief as younger mourners would. They may become victims of "disenfranchised grief."

In her book *Midlife Orphan*, freelance writer Jane Brooks reinforces this experience. Reporting on what she heard from many midlife orphans, she writes:

> Friends and coworkers do not comprehend or appreciate the magnitude of the loss of the last parent. The loss of a[n elderly] parent simply does not elicit the kind of empathy that other losses do. It's not that people aren't sympathetic, but had we lost a child, a sibling, or a spouse, our grief, however prolonged or protracted, would be more acceptable. When we don't get "back to normal" within a few weeks after the death of the last parent, we are suspect. Perhaps we were too attached to Mom or Dad. Maybe we were dependent or emotionally unstable. What else explains the prolonged mourning?[4]

Although this may be true in some cases, the vast majority of adults who lose both parents experience two primary reactions. First, as Miranda acknowledged, the loss of the last remaining parent puts us "on the front line," reminding us that "we are next." It forces us to confront our own mortality, if we haven't done so before. Second, as we have seen in other stories, one loss tends to trigger memories of prior losses. Many adults who lose one of their parents are so busy attending to the needs of the surviving parent that they don't entirely mourn the one who died. As a result, when the second parent dies, the emotional impact of both losses can be magnified. The adult child's realization of his or her changed status finally sinks in.

Linda: Connecting with Nature

Seekers, in awe of the universe and its complexity, are on a quest to understand their relationship to the universe, their fellow humans, and other forms of life. Linda shared with me how she did this by finding her connection with nature after the death of her husband. She said she initially "went through a nomadic state" in which she "would wander aimlessly about . . . trying to sense [her] relationship to the world." Since many of the people to whom Linda had been connected had now died, she described herself as feeling "very alone." To ease her loneliness, she sought refuge in nature—in particular, the trees visible from her window. In her words, she "decided to have a relationship with them and with God."

RESOLUTION

Her connection with nature filled the void in Linda's life by occupying the place that her husband had held for many years. While she initially found her path as a seeker, Linda still yearns for a companion with whom to share her life and hopes one day to find her dominant identity as a normalizer.

Josh: Finding Community and Belonging in Zen Buddhism

Josh's story demonstrates how the death of his father when Josh was seven influenced his life, as he first became a nomad and later a seeker. After his father died, Josh lived with his mother and older sister. As "the boy in [a] female-dominated household," Josh observed that he "had no male role model," no one to teach him "how to be a man." A painfully shy child with "few friends," Josh said he "didn't know how to make sense of the world." As time passed, Josh remained isolated, since his sister was "always busy with her friends and . . . boyfriend," and his mother held three jobs, which "didn't leave [her] too much time to listen" to Josh.

When he was nine, Josh's interest in Zen Buddhism was sparked by a public television program that depicted bearded, marijuana-smoking people "wearing berets and . . . black turtlenecks." Although at that age he had no idea these people were "beatniks," their lifestyle intrigued him enough to buy a book about it.

As Josh's experience illustrates, the death of a parent changes children's lives in many ways. The parent is lost not only as the children's provider but also as their role model and teacher. Often children feel that they have lost the desperately needed love and attention of their surviving parent as well. If children feel emotionally isolated, they may turn inward, unable to express their grief. Without a same-sex role model, children may also lose their sense of identity and of where they fit in their family and in their world.

Some children look outside the family or the immediate community for people with whom they can connect. Their performance in school might falter. They might hang around with other children who are not adequately supervised. Such children can be at risk for an array of emotional and behavioral problems.

Josh continued his journey as a nomad for several more years. He said he left for college "not knowing who I was or where I belonged," then kicked around for a time, first checking out the open land movement in Northern California. Quickly becoming discontented, he gravitated to San Francisco, which he described as a haven for "free spirits of all kinds—Hari Krishnas, Zen Buddhists, hippies, and flower children"—and became attracted to the Zen Center, "populated by lots of lost souls like myself."

The Zen monastery offered Josh what he termed "sustenance, a sense of family and community"; enabled him to hone his social skills; and provided "a male role model who in many ways replaced [his] father." He spent thirteen years at the monastery, eventually becoming ordained as a Buddhist priest. Following a scandal with the roshi (Zen master) that "blew the community apart," Josh found himself adrift once again and "had to figure out what to do next." When an acquaintance in the insurance industry suggested that Josh "could make a lot of money doing that," Josh said he "just sort of floated into" a financial services job. Although he described himself as "reasonably successful," the position "really didn't suit" him.

RESOLUTION

Josh spent almost ten years in transition again, searching for another Buddhist community, until national events prompted him to make a positive life-changing decision that enabled him to find resolution. During this period, Josh continued his Zen Buddhist practice. He also became politically active and grew increasingly discouraged with the United States' "conservative policies," which he saw as "harming Americans' lives."

When George W. Bush was, as Josh puts it, "handed the presidency by the Supreme Court," Josh "decided [he'd] had enough." Since his participation in retreats in Myanmar (Burma) and Thailand had enabled Josh to discover that he "felt much more simpatico with Asian people and their Buddhist practices," he moved to the predominantly Buddhist Thailand and resettled in "a small but cosmopolitan city" that is home to many expatriates.

Josh now enjoys what he calls "a modest life" in which he supports himself on his insurance residuals supplemented by English-teaching and translating jobs. He also travels around Southeast Asia, "practicing in different Buddhist communities." Josh sums up his present life by saying, "I feel freer than I have ever been."

Seekers such as Josh make a commitment to a community that not only shares their beliefs but also provides them with an identity, a purpose for their lives, and a sense of contentment that had previously eluded them.

Paula: Wisdom from Indigenous Culture

When Paula and I met, she was a successful professional woman, originally from Saint Louis, Missouri, who had become involved in business and political activities in Washington, D.C. Seven years before, her sixty-two-year-old father had succumbed after a two-and-a-half-year battle with a brain tumor.

Paula recalled that her father's diagnosis left her "in shock," since he "was the rock of the family" and had always been "a healthy, vital man" who seemed unlikely to die young. Paula described her father as "a hard fighter," whose initial reaction was that he was "not going to let it kill him." Although an operation failed to completely remove the tumor, Paula felt that the subsequent intensive course of radiation did prolong his life. Nine months before his death, her father's condition had deteriorated to the point that doctors decided to stop all treatments. Thereafter, Paula's mother cared for him at home for as long as she could; then hospice came in during his last few months.

Reminiscing about her father, Paula was able to appreciate the benefits of his dying process. She observed that "his development continued as he was becoming more impaired." Her father had been a newspaper editor, "who lived in his head and was an intellectual. His life was words—talking and reading." Paula noted that "his quality of life changed quickly" as his condition worsened and he became unable to speak, which she termed "a terrible loss for him." But her father never showed his feelings about the loss, choosing instead to "plo[w] right on."

While he could still walk, Paula's father "shifted his interests" and became devoted to gardening and to beautifying the yard. Even when he was confined to a wheelchair during his last six months, he continued visiting the arboretum to enjoy the flowers.

Paula told me that she and her father "got closer" over the course of his final illness, as she read to him and enjoyed listening to music with him. Noting that before his illness, her father couldn't stand the symphony and didn't even own a stereo, Paula said she now realized that his dying process gave him "the opportunity to do other things he never would have done," adding, "I think death is a time for growth, both for the dying person and the loved ones. My father's death set me on a spiritual path."

Before this experience, Paula said her view of death was "pretty conventional." She was not a spiritual person and admits she was afraid of death but gradually shifted her view of it. She is now much more conscious about living her life "every single day" and appreciates the limited time she has. Paula has come to believe "that the spirit separates from the body at death and that [her] father's spirit is either in the spirit world or has already gone on to another life incarnation." Observing that the "spirit knows things we don't," Paula feels that an ability to access and work with the spirit "would give us many resources."

Since Paula's parents were nontraditional in their religious beliefs (her father was born Jewish but became an atheist, and her mother was a nonpracticing Catholic), it was not surprising that Paula created her own spiritual path. Her exploration led her to the Peruvian Andes and the mysticism of the Q'ero Indians, descendants of the Incas, who have preserved their belief in the interconnectedness of the cosmos and their ancient spiritual practices. The Q'ero tradition requires that we see the world through our *hearts* rather than our *minds*, as is the case in the Judeo-Christian tradition. These ancient indigenous mystics of Peru maintain the customs of their Incan ancestors through three fundamental beliefs: Nature is alive and responsive. Spirit is present throughout the physical world. And the cosmos is a "vibrating field of pure energy."

RESOLUTION

During her treks to Machu Picchu and other sacred sites in Peru, Paula participated in the sacred ceremonies and listened to the shamans as they spoke of their prophecies for the spiritual evolution of mankind. She connected to spirit in the universe, holding her father's spirit in her heart. Paula says, "I believe his spirit is in the universe. If I need him, he will be there."

Marc: Escaping Pain, Rejecting the Past, and Creating a New Future

Some survivors who become seekers do so to escape family, friends, and other reminders of their painful past. Often their journey involves wandering as nomads, the way Josh did, before they find their spiritual path.

A fascinating article in the *Boston Globe*[5] caught my eye because it described an upcoming film at the Museum of Fine Arts in Boston that I had been planning to see. The film depicts the story of a father's sudden death from a heart attack and its traumatic impact on his surviving wife and their ten-year-old son and eight-year-old daughter. Twenty years later, the daughter, Julia Pimsleur, now a freelance filmmaker, decided to use the film as what she termed a way "to break the silence in [her] family."[6]

Her film, *Brother Born Again,* poignantly depicts her brother's journey from Judaism to Christianity, from New York to Alaska, and from the high-powered city life to the simplicity and certainty of a remote rural community called "The Farm." In her conversations with her brother, Julia found answers for what Christianity offered him. The *Boston Globe* article quoted Julia as saying:

> Our father was this strong and wonderful figure and one day he was not there. . . . I think God and Jesus represented father figures, rescuers. Marc was looking for salvation. Judaism is about questioning and searching, which is not a comfort when you want answers handed to you.[7]

Although Marc denied that his father's sudden death had affected him, other stories in this book provide evidence of how children's lives are transformed after the death of a parent.

Another interesting element in this story is how siblings can respond to the same loss so differently. "I am a filmmaker," Julia said. "This is my form of self-expression, so it made sense to use that."[8] In order to provide a balanced view of the unconventional choices each of them had made, Julia purposely discloses her bisexuality. She appears to be an activist, using her loss experience as a way to educate her audiences about appreciating lifestyle differences.

RESOLUTION

A positive outcome of Julia's film has been her reconciliation with her brother. Despite vastly different beliefs and lifestyles, they now have an unbreakable bond based on the tragic loss of their father and a deeper understanding of how his death influenced their choices for their lives. Furthermore, their stories, through Julia's film, will help others understand the deep and lifelong impact that a loved one's death can have on family members and other survivors.

Helen: Healing through an Alternative Path

Helen, a highly competent fifty-three-year-old single woman whose father died suddenly thirty-six years ago of a second heart attack when she was in her freshman year at college, described her initial reactions and how she evolved into a seeker. She said that after her father's death, she "channeled [her] energies into [her] studies at college" in order to maintain her eligibility for the scholarships she'd need in order to continue her education. During this period, Helen "became quite inner-directed," asking "why God could allow such things as death" and wondering, "Was I being punished?"

Having grown up in a community that left her feeling "marginalized," Helen developed what she termed "a victim consciousness." To protect herself "against the pain of further losses," Helen told me she "became independent to an extreme." No longer allowing herself to depend on anyone besides herself, she "decided to depend on the universe rather than on any individual." As the years passed, however, Helen became aware "that much of [her] identity was tied up with [her] career." When her job "started to crumble," Helen said she "felt so alone" and realized she faced a stark choice: "I [could] either . . . fall more deeply into depression or do something about it."

Deciding she "had to work on becoming 'interdependent' [and] learn to trust others," Helen joined what she described as "a healing group that 'channeled' spirit guides with others seeking to understand the challenges in their lives." Her participation in this group provided Helen with what she termed "an infrastructure" that hadn't been available to her at the time of her father's death. Her spiritual search led Helen to the realization "that others also experienced loss and that the universe was not singling me out." In Helen's words, "The most healing experience was knowing I was like everyone else."

RESOLUTION

These experiences taught Helen to trust others and acknowledge that her father's death was a valid part of life. It brought positive benefits she would not otherwise have received. Helen referred to Viktor Frankl's injunction that we should look to the positives, accept tragedy as a part of the human experience and move beyond it. She observed, "This tragedy tempered me a bit like steel, but it also made me appreciate life and sent me on a spiritual journey."

Helen's story illustrates how her loss helped her develop a spiritual path of exploration that connected her to communities of people to whom she could relate. Her father's death motivated her to look for solace in a higher power, the mark of a seeker with an outward perspective and a need for connection with the universe.

Of the five identity types, seekers may be considered unconventional in American society. Whether it is the commitment they make to connecting with a community of believers or the intensity with which they embrace their spiritual nature, the seekers' search for something beyond themselves is a quest for connection with the divine and its manifestation in them. This can be found in a variety of ways—awareness, prayer, meditation, and seeking guidance from religious or spiritual teachers. Each offers means of finding the answers to their questions about life.

Seekers come in many forms—the religious and the faithful—Catholics, Jews, Muslims, Hindus, and Buddhists, as well as ministers and rabbis, cult members, and New Age healers. Whoever asks these questions wonders about their relationship to the divine (however it is defined) or seeks comfort in their faith. Anne Lamott, herself a seeker whose father's death greatly influenced her writing, describes faith as a "way to bear the unbearable."[9]

Amish Forgiveness: The Massacre at Nickel Mines, Pennsylvania

In their book *Amish Grace: How Forgiveness Transcended Tragedy,* authors Donald B. Kraybill, Steven M. Nolt, and David L. Weaver-Zercher examine the belief in forgiveness as part of the theology and values of the Amish community.[10] After the 2006 tragedy in which a gunman ruthlessly murdered five schoolgirls and seriously wounded five others before killing himself, this long-standing community of faith astonished the world by demonstrating an "otherworldly" response to the calamity. They reached out to the killer's widow and children, attending his burial and donating money to her and her three young children.

The Amish have lived in America peacefully and separately in Pennsylvania, Ohio, and Indiana since the early eighteenth century, practicing a form of Christianity that believes that God will forgive them only if they forgive others. Jesus said, "Forgive, and you will be forgiven" (Luke 6:37).[11] However, the responsibility to forgive is not the individual's but the entire community's. The strong Amish community is providing support to the families of both the victims and the killer. The New Testament's command to "love your enemies" and their faith in God's plan allow the Amish to find serenity, observing of the victims that "their time was up, this was in God's Hands, and He will take care of them."[12]

ADVANTAGES OF BEING A SEEKER

Seekers understand the connectedness of all worldly things. They appreciate the value of life and the beauty of living every moment as a way of relating to the divine, however they may define it. Seekers think about the universality of the human experience. Among the five identity types, seekers are the sages, or wisdom seekers, open to new perspectives, ideas, and approaches. They contemplate what is really important in life and what is not.

Because seekers are searching for the meaning of life, they may perceive the loss of a loved one as a gift from which to learn and grow. They generally understand that death is the final stage of life and accept and even prepare for their own death with equanimity. However, they are more inclined than the other identity types to believe that after death, the person's soul or spirit lives on and that there is something beyond, offering continuity to life, whether it be heaven or reincarnation or what the *Tibetan Book of the Dead* describes as the "space the soul floats in" before going to the next life.[13]

Many seekers appreciate and adhere to the theology and traditions of the three major world religions—Christianity,

Judaism, and Islam—and spiritual philosophies, including Buddhism, Hinduism, and Taoism. They find comfort in the sense of community each offers. They turn to God or some "Higher Power" for guidance in meeting the challenges in their lives. Like these groups, seekers know they are not "in control" in life. The resulting ability to "let go" leads them on their path toward liberation—from anxieties, from stress, from material things. They strive for simplicity, authenticity, and morality in their lives and frequently have the support of a like-minded community of believers with whom to share their challenges and triumphs.

Seekers empathize with the human suffering of each individual as well as the human family. These characteristics tend to lead them to choose humanistic professions, such as health and medical care, humanities, or ministry, and academic interests in other cultures, religion, or mysticism.

DISADVANTAGES OF BEING A SEEKER

Although connectedness and a sense of community are so important for seekers, finding the right path can often be challenging. In addition to the inevitable differences in personality and human nature within any group, the nuances of spiritual practice also vary. While individual peace and universal harmony are desired goals for seekers, human foibles often interfere with achieving them. Seekers may feel frustrated and disillusioned by these realities, and idealism may be transformed into cynicism. These disappointments can be exacerbated by the environment in which seekers live. For example, the vestiges of New England's puritanical culture, in which relationships tend to be formal, reserved, and well defined, may be less comfortable for some seekers than the informal warmth and open-minded culture of a retreat center in Northern California. Seekers may have difficulty conforming to conventional norms, may be judged as "strange" or "far-out," and may have trouble finding a "place" in mainstream society where their philosophical or religious beliefs or practices are deemed acceptable.

STRATEGIES FOR HEALING AND GROWTH

If they are to heal from their loss and move forward, seekers must learn to *trust* other people. Many seekers who trust the universe have learned to do so as a way of compensating for the grave disappointments they experienced believing in those here on earth and in their immediate world. Parents who lose a child, children whose parents die, young widows—all must work to regain their trust in the world. They must learn to accept the foibles of others—family, friends, and lovers—and understand how the loss they suffered affected others as well.

In some cases, this may require that seekers revisit their past to reevaluate the trauma of their loss and the ways in which it contributed to their loss of trust in others. Psychotherapy or other forms of help, such as pastoral counseling or support groups, offer conventional methods of doing this. Other strategies from the repertoire of self-help systems, such as meditation, hypnosis, channeling, or past-life regression, may provide great support if they are more aligned with an individual's belief system.

Seekers may find communities in which to live, such as ashrams or monastic settings, ranches or farms, dedicated to a particular spiritual practice. Many organizations of like-minded individuals who share the seekers' beliefs and traditions may feel very welcoming and provide them with a comfortable setting in which to pursue their common interests. For those who do not choose a complete change of lifestyle to explore their spiritual interests, finding the right community is as close as the nearest library—or, in the Internet age, the nearest Web browser.

QUESTIONS FOR FURTHER EXPLORATION

As you have seen from reading the preceding chapters, I ask a series of questions at the end of each chapter to help you examine your story more closely. These questions are intended to help you understand how your loss has affected your life, and how your grief may be transformed into an opportunity for growth, meaning, and a new identity.

After reading this chapter, you may already have recognized yourself as a seeker. Or, perhaps you have had another identity, but believe the seeker represents the identity you would like to be. By contemplating the issues below, you may become clearer about where your true identity lies. Are you most like the seeker?

1. How do you make sense of your relationship between yourself, others, and the universe? What is your spiritual philosophy? Describe your religious or spiritual orientation and make a list of the beliefs about life and death that are related to it. Have they helped you heal as you have mourned the loss of your loved one?
2. How do you actively explore the meaning in life? List all the ways you've attempted to grapple with this question. How have these explorations benefited you?

For example, have you found new faith, new hope, or a community of like-minded people as a result?

3. What have you discovered in your journey toward meaning? How have these discoveries helped you make sense of your loss and your life? Why do you think you are so driven to understand the meaning of life?

4. Do you feel you don't know where you belong in this world? Are you frustrated or cynical with the way life is, and how people cope with grief and loss? Are there ways you have difficulty conforming to conventional norms in mainstream society?

5. How do you understand the relationship between the loss you experienced and the way you live your life now? Are you comfortable with the seeker identity?

REFLECTIONS FOR THE SEEKER

As a seeker, you are probably comfortable with asking yourself questions about the meaning of life. In fact, this exploration process probably helps you make some sense of the loss of your loved one. You probably are comfortable with the idea that we don't have control over much of our lives and feel secure in letting go of this misguided belief of individual control.

However, perhaps there are ways that in your seeking, you are not finding where you feel you belong. Perhaps this dissatisfaction has led to cynicism and frustration at the foibles of human life. Finding a community where you share spiritual beliefs and a home in the world is very important. Maybe there are ways for you to come to peace with the limitations of human life by adjusting your expectations. You may often feel disillusioned or disappointed by your spiritual communities as well.

There may not be a place where you find a perfect fit for you, but there may be a spiritual community that provides security and comfort and that you can call home.

Seven

Transforming Your Grief

Finding Your Personal Path to Healing

NOW THAT YOU ARE FAMILIAR with the five ways we grieve—as nomads, memorialists, normalizers, activists, and seekers—and have read the stories of other bereaved people, you can begin to transform your grief by stepping onto the path toward healing.

Everyone's grief is unique, and the grieving process happens in many ways. Healing reflects the healthy ways we adapt to our transformed life. It is a process that ebbs and flows over time, just as a physical injury heals gradually and over time. It is a process that requires you to *make a commitment to yourself.* In doing so, you may face some of the challenges that many survivors encounter in resolving their grief. Here are eight tips as you embark on this journey:

1. Accept the fact that resolving grief takes work, and it requires *feeling the pain.*
2. Recognize that denying the reality of the death, delaying the sadness, or blaming others will not help you heal.

3. Get to the bottom of your feelings toward the person you lost, such as sadness, anger, guilt, or fear, and work them through.

4. Find ways to adjust to an environment without your loved one.

5. Examine your loss experience—and how it has affected your worldview.

6. Contemplate these changes and what options you have for moving on with your life.

7. Make choices for how you can find meaning from your experience and stay connected to your loved one (if you want to).

8. Work toward creating your new identity and your new purpose in life.

HOW HAVE YOU CHANGED?
Reading and Thinking Activity

In reading about the five identity types, perhaps you've already found one that seems to describe you, or perhaps you have no idea which type you are.

In either case, I encourage you to participate in the following evaluation process, which asks you to reflect and describe. By the end of this process, you will have: (1) learned which identity type you are and (2) gained a deeper understanding of your experience of the grieving process. This exploration is a step toward transforming your sorrow into healing.

Treat yourself to an attractive notebook and pen and answer the questions in the following subsections. This is an opportunity for you to reflect on what you have learned about yourself. No one has to read this notebook except you, so be as candid as possible.

Don't worry about writing in complete sentences or polished prose. Instead, use this writing activity as a tool for thinking and for uncovering your ideas, feelings, and beliefs.

You might want to answer all the questions over a long weekend, or perhaps you'd prefer to address the questions individually, allowing time to pass between the steps.

Maybe you will want to reflect and write alone, or perhaps you will choose to write in the company of others.

You may want to process the experience with a supportive friend or therapist.

Or perhaps you can join a bereavement group, whether face-to-face or online, and go through these steps with other like-minded individuals.

The most important thing is to listen to your needs, be compassionate, and experiment to determine which process works best for you.

Step 1: Use the Four Pillars to Evaluate How Your Loss Has Changed Key Aspects of Your Worldview

When we suffer a devastating loss, our worldview shifts. The way we see the world is changed forever. In order to find out which identity type is closest to your experience of the grieving process, review and evaluate key aspects of your life before and after your loss in terms of the four pillars. Recall the four pillars as I defined them in the introduction:

1. Our sense of our own mortality
2. Our sense of time and orientation toward time
3. Our values and priorities regarding people and the world around us
4. Our relationship to the world

PILLAR ONE: OUR SENSE OF OUR OWN MORTALITY

Your feelings and beliefs about life and death are challenged by the loss of someone important to you. First, recall how you felt about life and death *before* your moment of loss, then ask yourself the following questions:

1. What were my beliefs about mortality?
2. Was I worried about how and when I would die?
3. Did I take life for granted?

Try to write more than just one-word answers. Call on your memories. Provide examples, explain, and expand on your answers. As you write, imagine you are talking to a caring friend—namely, you.

Now use the following questions to explore how your feelings about life and death may have changed *after* your loss:

1. Currently, what are my beliefs about mortality? Has my loss made me more aware of my own mortality? If it has, how and why? If it hasn't, why not?
2. Am I worried about how and when I will die?
3. Do I feel I take my life for granted now?

PILLAR TWO: OUR SENSE OF TIME AND ORIENTATION TOWARD TIME

Your sense of time may shift after a great loss. First, remember how you felt about time *before* your moment of loss, then ask yourself the following questions:

1. Did I focus on the past, the present, or the future?
2. As I lived my life before my loss, was I acutely aware of the passage of time?

3. Did I go with the flow of time, or did I feel that time was flying by?
4. Did I have a sense of urgency about what I wanted to do with the time allotted for my life?

Now use the following questions to explore how your feelings about time may have changed *after* your loss:

1. Do I tend to dwell on the past and wish my loved one were still here with me?
2. Do I accept the reality of my loss, live in the present, and appreciate the moment?
3. Do I believe that the way I live now through my choices and decisions will influence both my own future and the future of others?

PILLAR THREE: OUR VALUES AND PRIORITIES REGARDING PEOPLE AND THE WORLD AROUND US

Our values are the principles that guide our actions. These values, and the priorities based on them, influence our behaviors. Yet, despite the critical role of values in how we live our lives, we may be unaware that we hold a particular belief until it is challenged.

I challenge you to dig and identify your values and priorities. Start by listing what your values and priorities are in relation to the following concepts:

freedom

security

family

friendship

love

balance

community

work

relationships

risk

responsibility

justice

knowledge

connection

spirituality

creativity

loyalty

contribution

wisdom

Feel free to add and comment on any other fundamental concepts you regard as important.

Next, recall what your values and priorities were *before* your moment of loss, then ask yourself the following questions:

1. What were my values and priorities?
2. How did my values and priorities guide my actions and beliefs about what is important in my life?
3. How did my decisions and choices reflect my values and priorities?

Now use the following questions to explore how your values and priorities may have changed *after* your loss:

1. What are my values and priorities now? How have they changed?
2. How do my values and priorities now guide my actions and beliefs about what is important in my life?
3. How do my decisions and choices reflect my present values and priorities?

Pillar Four: Our Relationship to the World

After a loss, your sense of being safe and secure in the world may shift. Your relationship to God, a Higher Power, or other spiritual energy may also be disrupted, challenged, or forced to change. Remember your relationship to the world as it was *before* your moment of loss, then ask yourself the following questions:

1. Did I believe that the world was a good and safe place? Did I feel secure?
2. Did I trust in God or hold some other spiritual beliefs?
3. Where was I most comfortable being?
4. What did I feel was my place in the world?

Now use the following questions to explore how your relationship to the world may have changed *after* your loss:

1. Do I still believe that the world is a good and safe place? Do I continue to feel secure?
2. Do I trust in God or hold some other spiritual beliefs?
3. Where am I most comfortable being?
4. What is my place in the world now?

Step 2: Describe the Change in Your Worldview

Read over what you've written in response to the questions in step 1, and write an assessment based on what you've discovered about yourself.

Here are some questions to ponder:

1. Has my worldview changed since I experienced my loss? If it has changed, describe how. (Provide some specific examples.) If it hasn't changed, explain why not.
2. Have my feelings, beliefs, and behavior changed? If they've changed, explain how and why. If they haven't changed, explain why not.

Step 3: Identify Your Personal Path to Healing

After reviewing the identity types described earlier in this book, ask yourself the following questions:

1. Do one or more of the five identity types depict the ways in which I have approached the grieving process?
2. With which identity type do I identify the most closely?
3. Does this identity offer me the *possibility* of creating a new and meaningful purpose in life without my loved one? If not, what is still holding me back in my grief?
4. Does this identity provide a guide that would enable me to move on with my life? If not, what is still holding me back in my grief?

Step 4: Examine Your "Identity Hang-ups"

Identity hang-ups are feelings and beliefs that may be holding you back from healing. For example:

- *Feelings:* anger, guilt, sadness, fear
- *Beliefs:* I am being punished. I don't deserve to be happy. It was my fault. I didn't do enough. I can't believe this has happened.

List all your identity hang-ups.

Step 5: Explore Ways That You Can Work on Healing Your Grief

Survivors of loss can work toward healing their grief in many ways, including:

1. Using do-it-yourself approaches:
   - Read books.
   - Write in a journal.
   - Exercise.
   - Keep busy.
   - Join a group to meet new people.
   - Develop new interests you haven't had time to pursue before.
   - Explore spirituality: prayer, meditation, contemplation, or yoga.
   - Express your grief—cry, scream, or punch a pillow.
   - Find a good friend in whom to confide.

2. Seeking help from other laypeople:
   - Join an online chat room for grievers who have experienced a similar kind of loss.
   - Attend bereavement support groups to find other survivors who can understand what you are going through.
   - Join activities with others who have experienced similar losses.

3. Seeking help from professionals:
   - Attend individual therapy and/or group therapy to deal with the emotional, cognitive, and behavioral aspects of grieving.
   - Consult your doctor about physical symptoms related to grief.
   - Explore complementary and alternative medical practices, such as acupuncture, yoga, or aromatherapy, to use in conjunction with standard medical care.
   - Consult a spiritual advisor at your church or synagogue.

WHO ARE YOU NOW?

Discovering your new identity after your loved one dies is one of the most difficult challenges in the grieving process. Since who we are—whether it be a parent, child, spouse, or sibling—is often defined in relation to our loved one, his or her death requires us to define ourselves in a new way and live without that person in a changed reality. The preceding five steps may help you determine who you are *now*.

You should be aware that the process of finding a new identity normally evolves throughout our lives. We may adopt different identities at various points in our lives, based on our relationship to our lost loved one. I want to emphasize, however, that each of us who loses a loved one need not experience *every one* of the five identities in order to find our path to healing. Nor do these five ways to grieve represent a continuum from beginning to end. Each of the identities is unique, with its own strengths and weaknesses.

As I concluded from my research, and as the stories of survivors in this book demonstrate, every individual assumes a *dominant* identity—as a nomad, a memorialist, a normalizer, an activist (the path I chose), or a seeker—based on his or her sense of mortality, perspective on time, values and priorities, and relationship to the world. What is your dominant identity?

As things change over time, however, survivors might respond in one of two ways: First, they could shift into a nomad identity during a period of crisis and then return to their dominant identity. Second, since grieving is a lifelong process, they could evolve positively in relation to their loss and discover a new identity that they decide is more authentic for them. These are both acceptable ways of healing. My concern is for the survivors who don't adequately resolve their grief issues, since they are likely to find themselves as nomads again and again.

Eight

Hope for the Future

I need a hope . . . a new hope
A hope that inspires me to live. . . .
> —Mattie Stepanek, poet, peacemaker, and
> philosopher (mattieonline.com)

I HOPE THAT READING the earlier chapters has given you a better understanding of how deeply complex the death of a loved one can be and that this knowledge allows you to feel compassion for yourself about how your life has been affected. You should understand that your life is different, you are different. You have faced new challenges. You have had to redefine yourself and your place in your family, your community, and the larger world. You may have felt the sting of rejection from friends and acquaintances who view you differently or feel uncomfortable being around you. You may have felt people's impatience with your inability to shake off your feelings of sadness or anger, confusion or loneliness— even years after your loved one's death. They just want you to move on with your life. And, even if you have moved on, you may feel that you've only been going through the motions, unfulfilled, with no real meaning for your life.

You have read the stories of many survivors who have gone through the intense pain of loss and have converted their grief into a way of remaining connected to their loved ones while creating new meaning and purpose for their own lives. They have found new identities as memorialists, normalizers, activists, or seekers. Using their stories as guides for your life may give you the opportunity to discover untapped aspects of yourself that can help you transform yourself and heal from your grief, regardless of whether that grief is fresh or something you have been carrying around for years.

SHORT-TERM IMPACT OF LOSS

If your loved one died within the last year, you may identify most closely with the nomad identity and the acute stage of the grieving process. Grief is a normal reaction to loss. Everyone feels grief. Being left behind after the death of someone we love leaves us in a state of deprivation called *bereavement*. Like infants and young children who feel intense distress at being separated from their mothers, adults also feel a sense of vulnerability about what our life will be like as we face it alone.

The tales of nomads I have shared with you are intended to help you to understand how normal grieving may become "complicated grieving" if the issues related to loss are not addressed with guidance from concerned family members and friends, support groups, or professionals. As we have seen, however, these survivors need not remain nomads. With help, nomads can find a new path to healing.

LONG-TERM IMPACT OF LOSS

If you have lived for years, as I did, with a cloud hovering over your head, I hope that the accounts of more than sixty survivors have demonstrated how losing their loved ones inspired them to transform themselves and create a new sense of purpose and identity. You have seen how their worldview shifted through what I term the four pillars: their sense of mortality, their perception of time, their values and priorities for living, and their relationship to the world. You have witnessed how their lives and their characters were forever changed by their trauma.

You met Eileen, whose early loss of her father prompted her to become an activist and commit herself to social justice for all. You observed Myrim, the Israeli artist who chose to become a memorialist, adapting his superb welding skills to crafting magnificent metalworks as a tribute to his son killed in the Yom Kippur War. You saw how they and so many other survivors moved beyond being nomads, the initial identity of most grievers. They transformed their grief by creating meaning from their loss and healed themselves by gradually adopting one of the other four identities.

FINDING YOUR NEW IDENTITY

Most of the men and women with whom I spoke while collecting their stories expressed how they had made meaning from their loss (except for the nomads, who had not yet figured this out). Although each of their responses was unique, every one carried a positive message that helped the person make sense of a tragic experience. Making sense of their loss enabled these mourners to transform their grief into a new identity and gave them a meaningful purpose in life. For example:

MEMORIALISTS

- "My son did not die in vain. I will assure that he is remembered." (Ken, age forty-seven)
- "My wife loved gardening, so I am dedicating this healing place to her." (Bill, whose story appears in the "Healing Garden" subsection of chapter 3)

NORMALIZERS

- "I loved being married, and I want to enjoy that kind of love and companionship again." (Octavia, whose story appears in chapter 4)
- "I want to give my children the family life I lost." (Carl, age forty-nine, whose story appears in chapter 4)

ACTIVISTS

- "My wife made a difference in other people's lives, and I will continue her efforts." (Mark, age sixty-two)
- "I want to help others as I was supported through my grief." (Ann, whose story appears in chapter 5)

SEEKERS

- "My father's death brought me closer to God." (Jeremy, age thirty-five)
- "I have found a place to belong, to share my values and beliefs, and feel protected." (Sarah, age twenty-seven)

USING MEANING-MAKING TO HELP YOU
DISCOVER YOUR NEW IDENTITY

The preceding quotations from survivors offer examples of how people make sense of losing a loved one. They may not have all the answers to the practical aspects of their loved one's death, such as the final event that caused the death, the mistakes that could have been avoided, the bad luck that couldn't have been foreseen. They may never know why this misfortune—the illness, the accident, the catastrophe—was visited on their loved one. But they have moved beyond this fruitless line of questioning. What's important to these individuals now is reexamining their worldview, as it has been defined in this book; identifying what's really important to them in life; and discovering what lessons can be learned that might help them grow as a result of their tragedy.

As we have discussed here, the major challenges for survivors are finding meaning from their loss and creating a new identity. In most (though not all) cases, this identity will reinforce their attachment to their loved one and enable them to find the significant link from their loved one's life that will help them remain connected in their *heart* even as they continue living without their loved one. Robert Neimeyer eloquently expresses this process:

> Making meaning of these life transitions entails a delicate interplay between explicit redefinition of our identities as spouses, parents, sons and daughters, in light of this dislodgement, and an implicit reweaving of our ways of anticipating and engaging in the world.[1]

As we have seen, for those who did not enjoy a positive relationship with the person they lost, these challenges remain. Everyone must adapt to the loss of the relationship; everyone must find a new identity by understanding the meaning of the loss. These tasks are essential in order to avoid the unresolved grief that leads to complicated grieving. Resolution allows us to rekindle the sense of hope we need to reinvest in living.

BOTH SURVIVING AND THRIVING BY FINDING HOPE FOR THE FUTURE

Many of you reading this book may be familiar with Matthew Stepanek, a thirteen-year-old boy who became renowned for his poetry and writings about hope and peace. Afflicted with a rare and fatal form of muscular dystrophy, he inspired millions of Americans with his hopes and dreams, despite knowing he would likely die before they would come to fruition. As Dr. Jerome Groopman, a Boston oncologist, journalist, and author, wrote in *The Anatomy of Hope:* "To have hope under extreme circumstances is an act of defiance that permits a person to live life on his or her own terms."[2] To me, Mattie was the embodiment of hope that the world could be a better place.

The element of hope has been implicit throughout this book. Grief often deprives us of hope. We feel despair. We feel that there is nothing left to live for, that we have lost our purpose in life. But if we successfully complete the grieving process by finding meaning from our loss, and we pursue a new sense of self that includes a continuing bond to our deceased loved one, we can transform our grief into hope for the future.

Although hope draws on the past, it is focused on the future. When psychiatrist Viktor Frankl, in *Man's Search for Meaning,* distinguishes between those in the Nazi concentration camps who survived and those who did not, he attributes the major difference to hope.[3] Holocaust victims endured the most extreme trauma and grief imaginable. Those who developed an inner life, envisioning music and art, or those who found humor, however fleeting, in some facet of their situation—these individuals generated internal stamina that preserved them. Those of us who hold on to hope for the future after our loved one dies are likely not only to survive but also to thrive and appreciate life more fully, despite the dire circumstances of our loss.

Frankl's personal technique of mentally conversing with his wife was a common practice among his fellow prisoners. During the early morning forced marches to the worksite, the prisoners proceeded

> in the darkness, over big stones and through large puddles, [being driven] with the butts of [the guards'] rifles. . . . The man marching next to me whispered suddenly: "If our wives could see us now! I do hope they are better off in their camps and don't know what is happening to us."[4]

When daily suffering and threats of the gas chambers loomed so large, what was significant in this man's imagining their wives? It is that as long as we are alive, humans are capable of forming images of what is possible, visualizing a better future, and creating a path to reach it. As Helen Keller observed, "In dreams we catch glimpses of a life larger than our own."[5]

This brings us to the final stage of your journey through grief to healing. You acknowledge that the loss of a loved one is an experience that is final, life-altering, and beyond your control. You will be changed by your loss whether you like it or not. You cannot alter the fact of his or her death. How you go on with your life and how you manage the impact of your loss, however, are very much within your control. You *can* work with finding a way to transform your life so that you may live a happier, more productive, fulfilling, and compassionate existence. You can live in a way that honors your loved one's memory by doing what he or she would want you to do.

You can make decisions based on your attitude and approach to life after your loss. You can choose either to be a victim of your misfortune or to discover meaning from it. You can survive at a minimal level of functioning, or you can adapt to your new world and continue to grow. I believe that Dr. Groopman's words offer considerable encouragement:

> Hope can arrive only when you recognize that there are real options and that you have genuine choices. Hope can flourish only when you believe that what you do can make a difference, that your actions can bring a future different from the present. To have hope, then, is to acquire a belief in your ability to have some control over your circumstances. You are no longer entirely at the mercy of forces outside yourself.[6]

You must go through a process of reflection, self-exploration, and questioning of your innermost beliefs and values. Every aspect of your life—self, family, friends, and community—may require revision. You may decide to alter your worldview. This quest requires considerable energy—emotional, mental, spiritual, as well as physical—to construct a new reality for yourself and your life.

Life must be lived for some reason, so finding an answer to the question "Who am I now?" is the goal of your journey through the grieving process. John McAfee, yoga master and teacher of self-discovery techniques, offers the following advice:

It is through questioning, with the burning desire to know the answer, that the truth is revealed. And it is ourselves whom we must question. This questioning of ourselves is the only road to a full healing.[7]

Creating a new identity that reflects the sense you make of your loss and the meaning you can draw from it might seem an intimidating challenge. Having read through this book, however, I hope that you have gained the knowledge, confidence, and desire to find your personal path to healing. Healing *is* possible. You may feel despair or deep pain, but the fact that you have picked up this book is evidence that you believe your healing is within reach. How can you grow that little glimmer of hope inside you to something that will beam wide rays of sunshine?

I pose a challenge to you, my readers: Find the opening in your heart and mind to question yourself, to critically evaluate the life you have now and ask yourself:

- Am I living the life I want?
- Have the deaths I have experienced colored my view of the world in positive or negative ways?
- Can I have a richer, more meaningful, and more satisfying life?
- What do I need to do to change my life?
- I encourage you to embrace hope for your future and *take control of your own grieving process.*

You have the power to develop a new identity that can alter your destiny in positive ways instead of floating along without direction or settling for things the way they are.

You have read about the five identity types and the four pillars. Perhaps you highlighted passages as you read the book. Maybe you made notes in the margins or in a note-book. I hope you considered the questions I posed at the end of each identity type chapter. Now is the time to recall your memories, your feelings, and the decisions you have made about your life. Then respond to the following questions:

- Can you pinpoint the identity type that describes you now?
- Are you satisfied with that identity?
- Does it offer you the opportunities you desire to find purpose in your life?
- If not, what steps should you take to change? What decisions must you make?
- Are you ready to do so?

If your answer to the last question is "Yes!" you are ready to use the road map this book provides to find your path to healing. You may need to read the book more than once. You may want to work with a partner, a friend, or a fam-ily member to reflect on chapters, sections, or stories that especially resonate with you. You may want to discuss cer-tain issues with a therapist. The goal of this activity is to find freedom by expressing your grief rather than keeping it inside and feeling isolated and alone. The outcome of your efforts is your transformation into the person you want to be after your loss. Reaching your destination is up to you.

The path from mourning to healing is not straight and narrow but rather oscillates from memories of your past to accommodation to the future. These swings are less predict-able than the rhythmic ebb and flow of ocean tides, involving emotional highs and lows that, over time, gradually carry us forward into a new chapter of our life. Those who success-fully endure this grieving process define a new relationship to their loved one, forge a new path to discovering and creating their new or reaffirmed identity. They become able to reinvest in the world with a sense of hope and purpose.

When I began writing this book, I did not realize I was embarking on a personal journey that would take almost ten years. While I was motivated to learn from others about the long-term impact of the death of a loved one on their lives, I was also searching for answers for my own life: to bring to conscious awareness how my father's death, and later my mother's, had affected my entire life and gain insights about why I am who I am and why my life is what it has been.

I hope you have learned that understanding your own responses to loss can help you to evaluate the choices you have made and the identity you have chosen or wish to have. This book can empower you to live with greater intention in your postloss life. It's your life. How are you going to make the most of it? Who are you going to be?

Conclusion

Support for Your Healing

No man is an island, entire of itself. . . . Any man's death diminishes me, because I am involved in Mankind; and therefore never send to know for whom the bell tolls; it tolls for thee.

—"Meditation XVII," John Donne,
Renaissance poet, priest, and preacher

THE PURPOSE OF THIS BOOK is to help all of you who have lost a loved one to use the sadness of loss to find ways to live a more meaningful life. As you have seen, the book is unique because it guides people in the process of developing a new identity and finding a new path to healing. Your challenge is to explore the potential of these "five ways" in which we grieve in order to carve out a new way of being in the world. Each of you has many choices about the person you become, and although the loss of a loved one is unquestionably traumatic, it carries with it hidden gifts as well.

HIDDEN GIFTS OF LOSS

Judith Viorst, psychoanalyst and author of *Necessary Losses*, writes that losses are crucial in order for us to grow and that since we cannot change the losses, we have to "choose what to do with our dead."[1] This book has presented the stories of many remarkable bereaved individuals who have survived their losses. Most of them (except for the nomads) have found ways to deal with their dead and find meaning from the death of their loved one. As Robert Neimeyer claims, this mastery is critical to the successful reconstruction of a person's identity and long-term recovery.[2] In most cases (again, except for the nomads), the bereaved created an identity that enabled them to stay connected to their loved ones, allowing the deceased to remain an integral part of the survivors' lives. They have found their unique path to healing.

Another "unsought benefit" is suggested by Joan Borysenko, a leader in the psychology of mind-body healing. "In order for our suffering to have any meaning at all," she writes, "it must ultimately increase the capacity of all humankind both to love and be loved."[3] She recounts the tragic accidental death of Mat, a friend of her son Andrei, and the bonding that occurred between their families afterward. She concludes that Andrei "responded to Mat's death with a deep sorrow that ripened into an increased gratitude for life and a powerful realization that loving relationships are the most precious thing we can aspire to."[4] Her thoughts are reminiscent of many of the ideas we have read here of Viktor Frankl, who instructed us that "meaning becomes available through suffering"[5] and urged us to understand the importance of living for the future as a way of transcending present reality.

CONNECTEDNESS AS AN
ANTIDOTE TO GRIEF

When we lose a loved one, fear is one of the strongest emotions we feel. Fear for our safety and our basic security. Fear about what will happen to us and our family. Fear of not being able to manage our responsibilities on our own. Fear of being alone. When we feel connectedness to others and to the universe, however, we will not feel fear because, as Borysenko tells us, "Fear cannot exist where there is connectedness because the core of fear is isolation."[6]

So many people think that their feelings of grief are unique, that no one can understand their agony. Whether you are hurting from decades-old memories or aching from a recent loss, I assure you that you are not alone. The death of a loved one is such a personal event. Yet Donne's words remind us that we are all interconnected. Grief is to be shared with others, perhaps to lessen the burden on the mourners themselves or to remind us that grief is a universal experience.

As a result, innumerable resources are available in the community, online, in libraries, in bookstores, and in the media. They can provide you with the support you need to help you deal with your loss and make the choices necessary for your new life. These resources include nonprofit organizations, support groups, churches and synagogues, colleges and universities. An array of bereavement resources also exists at the state and national level to assist you in dealing with the issues of your loss. Whether you call them on the phone or access them on your computer, each of these resources can help bring you closer to resolving your grief, to finding and achieving your new identity and purpose. These resources are listed in appendix 2.

Extensive support exists to provide you with the knowledge, tools, and inspiration to find your personal path to healing. Now it is up to you. Despite the devastating effects of loss on you and your life, you can transform yourself and discover a new life of meaning and purpose. I hope this book will help.

Appendix One

About the Interviews

THE MEN AND WOMEN who participated in my story collection ranged in age from twenty-four to sixty-five at the time of the interviews. Forty were women and twenty men, mainly because, as many researchers in the field of death and bereavement have found, women are more open to discussing their experiences of death and loss than men. Sixteen had suffered the loss of their fathers before reaching adulthood. Seven had lost their mothers, three in their teen years. Of this group, six interviewees had lost both parents before reaching middle age. Of those who lost spouses, eleven had lost husbands; five had lost their wives. Two women lost fiancés. Two women and one man lost their teenage sons. Two participants had stillborn baby girls, one who succumbed to a rare condition, the other whose cause of death was never determined. One woman lost her young adult brother. Another lost a young adult nephew. Two women had lost grandfathers. One woman lost a grandchild.

The majority of the deaths were due to various forms of cancer (including brain tumors), heart failure, or complications from diabetes. Most were anticipated, though several occurred suddenly and without warning. One death resulted from polio before the vaccine virtually eliminated this disease; another was due to Alzheimer's, for which a cure is still being sought. Several deaths resulted from violent occurrences, including the terrorist attack on the World Trade Center in New York on September 11, 2001. Two deaths resulted from motor vehicle–related accidents. Another involved a father's suicide by self-inflicted gunshot. In several other deaths, alcoholism was a probable contributing factor.

Everyone whom I interviewed was self-selected. That is, the interviewees approached me upon learning about my research or were referred by someone who also had been interviewed.

Given my objective to learn about the long-term impact of loss, my key criterion for participation in the study was that the loss had to have occurred at least five years prior to the interview and that the participants had to be adults. In fact, 90 percent of the respondents had experienced their losses ten, fifteen, or twenty years earlier, making their long-term perspective valuable and relevant for me and my readers. However, two were affected by the attacks of September 11, 2001, and were included after three years. My judgment was that their experiences would add value to the book.

There were several members from three families. Respondents came predominantly from northeastern states (Massachusetts, New Hampshire, Maine, and New Jersey), the mid-Atlantic region (Maryland; Washington, D.C.; and North Carolina), and California. One was Asian-American. Two were Israelis. The interviewees constituted a well-educated, Caucasian, middle-class sample of individuals from the business world and various professions, though I would have wished for more diversity had the opportunities arisen. I acknowledge that this was not a scientific sampling method, but as the experience of several research colleagues has confirmed, it is not always easy to find people willing to expose themselves and their feelings about death and loss. What was important was to capture the stories of individuals whose experiences represented a wide range of types and causes of loss so that readers could relate to them based on their own experiences. I believe I succeeded in achieving this goal.

In order to make my respondents as comfortable as possible, I met them at times and in locations that were informal and accessible for them—my office, their offices, their homes, or in several cases, the nearest Starbucks. Although I was interested in letting them tell me their stories, I had a short questionnaire that I presented to everyone, requesting demographic information about the survivor, the deceased, and family members; cause and circumstances of death; and length of time since death. In addition, all respondents were asked to describe their overall worldview as a result of their loss, through open-ended questions about their views of life and death. I asked how their loss had influenced their sense of their own mortality, their values and priorities, the choices they had made in their life, and how they perceived their relationship to other people and the world around them.

I recorded each of our conversations with the respondents' permission, then transcribed the tape recordings, cross-referencing them with written notes I had taken. Depending on the person, the length of each interview varied from about one hour to two and a half hours. I also transcribed the responses to the questionnaires mentioned above. Because the questions in both the interviews and the questionnaires were open-ended, the data provided sufficient material for me to identify themes and patterns of responses that emerged from the answers.

Through this exploration, I found that people do change their perspective on life, the way they see the world and their place in it. Most survivors revise their values and priorities about what is important. Whether consciously or not, they make choices about how to live going forward. I discovered that those who successfully survived their loss created a new relationship to their loved one, made meaning from their loss, and reinvested in the world with a new sense of hope and purpose. In doing so, they created a new identity.

The themes that appeared led me to define five "identities" that survivors adopt after their loss. The nomad does not understand or acknowledge that he or she has no clear identity. The remaining identities offer bereaved readers four distinct potential paths for finding a meaningful purpose and healing in their postloss life.

Resources for Self-Help

Books

Black, Claudia. *Changing Course: Healing from Loss, Abandonment and Fear.* 2nd ed. Center City, Minn.: Hazelden, 1999.

Borysenko, Joan. *Fire in the Soul: A New Psychology of Spiritual Optimism.* New York: Warner Books, 1993.

Brener, Anne. *Mourning & Mitzvah: A Guided Journal for Walking the Mourner's Path through Grief to Healing.* Woodstock, Vt.: Jewish Lights Publishing, 1993.

Bridges, William. *Transitions: Making Sense of Life's Changes.* 2nd ed. New York: Da Capo Press, 2004.

———. *The Way of Transition: Embracing Life's Most Difficult Moments.* Cambridge, Mass.: Perseus Publishing, 2001.

Brooks, Jane. *Midlife Orphan: Facing Life's Changes Now That Your Parents Are Gone.* New York: Berkley Books, 1999.

Chethik, Neil. *FatherLoss: How Sons of All Ages Come to Terms with the Deaths of Their Dads.* New York: Hyperion, 2001.

Doka, Kenneth, ed. *Living with Grief after Sudden Loss: Suicide, Homicide, Accident, Heart Attack, Stroke*. Washington, D.C.: Hospice Foundation of America, 1996.

Edelman, Hope. *Motherless Daughters: The Legacy of Loss*. Reading, Mass.: Addison-Wesley Publishing Company, 1994.

Estés, Clarissa Pinkola. *The Creative Fire: Myths and Stories on the Cycles of Creativity*. Audiobook. Louisville, Colo.: Sounds True, 2005.

Frankl, Viktor E. *Man's Search for Meaning*. New York: Washington Square Press, 1959.

Groopman, Jerome. *The Anatomy of Hope: How People Prevail in the Face of Illness*. New York: Random House, 2004.

———. *The Measure of Our Days: New Beginnings at Life's End*. New York: Viking Press, 1997.

Harris, Jill Werman, ed. *Remembrances and Celebrations: A Book of Eulogies, Elegies, Letters, and Epitaphs*. New York: Pantheon Books, 1999.

Harris, Maxine. *The Loss That Is Forever: The Lifelong Impact of the Early Death of a Mother or Father*. New York: Penguin Books, 1996.

Kingsolver, Barbara. *Prodigal Summer*. New York: HarperCollins, 2000.

Krauss, Pesach, with Morrie Goldfischer. *Why Me? Coping with Grief, Loss and Change*. New York: Bantam Books, 1988.

Kushner, Harold S. *When Bad Things Happen to Good People*. New York: Avon Books, 1981.

Levang, Elizabeth. *When Men Grieve: Why Men Grieve Differently & How You Can Help*. Minneapolis: Fairview Press, 1998.

McLeod, Beth Witrogen. *Caregiving: The Spiritual Journey of Love, Loss, and Renewal*. New York: Wiley, 1999.

Rando, Therese A. *How to Go on Living When Someone You Love Dies*. New York: Bantam Books, 1991.

Rosof, Barbara D. *The Worst Loss: How Families Heal from the Death of a Child*. New York: Henry Holt and Company, 1994.

Secunda, Victoria. *Losing Your Parents, Finding Your Self: The Defining Turning Point of Adult Life*. New York: Hyperion, 2000.

Simon, Clea. *Fatherless Women: How We Change after We Lose Our Dads*. New York: Wiley, 2001.

Styron, William. *Darkness Visible: A Memoir of Madness*. New York: Vintage Books, 1990.

Surya Das, Lama. *Awakening the Buddha Within: Tibetan Wisdom for the Western World*. New York: Broadway Books, 1997.

———. *Awakening to the Sacred: Creating a Spiritual Life from Scratch*. New York: Broadway Books, 1999.

Tatelbaum, Judy. *The Courage to Grieve: Creative Living, Recovery, and Growth through Grief*. New York: Harper & Row, 1980.

Selected Organizations

The following resources are both general and specific. They are intended for all survivors of loss. Some Web sites specifically address parents who have lost infants, children, and teens; others address children who have lost parents and siblings; others, widows and widowers; and others, victims of violence such as murder, combat, and disasters; and others address survivors of suicide.

General Grief

Centering Corporation provides access to grief literature available through the Web.

> Centering Corporation
> 7230 Maple Street
> Omaha, NE 68134
> (866) 218-0101
> www.centering.org

Growth House is a comprehensive resource offering a wide range of grief information, as well as on end-of-life issues.

> Growth House
> 2215-R Market Street #199
> San Francisco, CA 94114
> (415) 863-3045
> www.growthhouse.org

Grief Recovery Online offers message boards, chat groups, and online resources, including Spanish language groups.

> Grief Recovery Online in the United States:
> POB 6061-382
> Sherman Oaks, CA 91413
> (818) 907-9600

> Grief Recovery Online in Canada:
> RR1
> St. Williams, Ontario
> Canada NOE 1PO
> (519) 586-8825

> www.groww.org

GriefNet.org is an Internet community of people dealing with grief, death, and major loss. It provides access to approximately fifty e-mail support groups for children and their families, veterans, and special memorials such as Hurricane Katrina, September 1, 2001, and London, July 7, 2005.

GriefNet
POB 3272
Ann Arbor, MI 48106-3272
www.griefnet.org

Mount Ida College houses the National Center for Death Education. It has an extensive library on thanatology topics, and offers workshops and summer seminars for grief counselors and health and mental health professionals.

National Center for Death Education (NCDE)
Mount Ida College
777 Dedham Street
Newton, MA 02459
(617) 928-4649
ncde@mountida.edu
www.mountida.edu/sp.cfm?pageid=307

Bereaved Spouses

WidowNet, established in 1995, is the first online information and self-help resource for and by men and women of different ages, religions, and sexual preferences, who have suffered the loss of a spouse or life partner.

www.widownet.org

The AARP offers grief and loss programs, particularly for widowed persons.

American Association of Retired Persons (AARP)
601 E Street NW
Washington, DC 20049
(888) 687-2277
www.aarp.org/life/griefandloss

Bereaved Parents

The Compassionate Friends
900 Jorie Blvd., Suite 78
Oak Brook, IL 60523
Toll-free (877) 969-0010
www.compassionatefriends.org

Bereaved Parents of the USA provides information and support for parents, grandparents, and siblings, especially the newly bereaved.

Bereaved Parents of the USA
P.O. Box 95
Park Forest, IL 60466
(708) 748-7866
www.bereavedparentsusa.org

The M.I.S.S. Foundation: Mothers in Sympathy and Support

P.O. Box 5333
Peioria, AZ 85385-5333
www.misschildren.org

The Missing Grace Foundation for pregnancy and infant loss.

(763) 497-0709
info@missinggrace.org
www.missinggrace.org

The National Organization of Parents of Murdered Children

National POMC
100 East Eighth Street
Suite 202
Cincinnati, OH 45202
(888) 818-POMC
www.pomc.org

Bereaved Children

The Dougy Center for Grieving Children and Families was one of the first organizations in the country dedicated to helping children, teens, their families, and adult caregivers grieve a death. It offers support services including training and training manuals for developing community-based grief programs, videos, books, and other information especially for children.

The Dougy Center
P.O. Box 86852
Portland, OR 97286
(866) 775-5683
help@dougy.org
www.dougy.org

National Organizations

Alzheimer's Association National Office
225 N. Michigan Avenue, 17th floor
Chicago, IL 60601
(800) 272-3900
www.alz.org

American Association of Suicidology
5221 Wisconsin Avenue NW
Washington, DC 20015
(202) 237-2280
www.suicidology.org

Association for Death Education and Counseling
111 Deer Lake Road, Suite 100
Deerfield, IL 60015
(847) 509-0403
www.adec.org

Healing Arts

As valuable as the above resources are for helping us understand and cope with our grief, I believe that in order to heal, we must also touch our souls. The spirit within us defines us as more than rational and physical beings, but also as spiritual creatures who search for meaning in our lives. As we have seen throughout this book, the experience of grief intensifies this quest and provides the context for our growth in all aspects of our humanity.

I have found that through creative expression, whether it is writing, music, fine arts, or performance, we come closer to our souls when we connect with the arts. Therefore, I am suggesting the following ways to reflect, meditate, and find your own inspiration for healing.

Albert Lee Strickland's article, "The Healing Power of Music," in *The Forum* (Association of Death Education and Counseling, April/May/June 2003, www.adec.org/coping), discusses the numerous ways that music of all kinds provides comfort and hope to the bereaved.

Webhealing.com is an interactive Web site with more than two thousand registered members. This site offers survivors the opportunity to tell their stories on an "Honor Page." The act of writing is a creative process, and the site provides a safe place for people to express their grief, and receive support and comfort from others.

www.webhealing.com

Anne Milligan's Hospice Ritual offers music composed for families to honor loved ones who have died through a musical format called "The Flow of Life." Information is presented in English and Spanish.

Anne Milligan, LCSW
POB 22824
Louisville, KY 40252
www.annemilligan.com/hospiceritual.html

Griefsong, and specifically Meditation Healing displays the vocal accomplishments of Paul Alexander, a social worker in a children's hospice program, who has experienced personal loss. His broad musical programs offer beautiful melodies for reflection and inspiration as well as faith-based and liturgical songs and instrumentals in the Catholic and Christian traditions. One song, "Who Am I Now?" reflects the question every survivor asks after losing a loved one.

Paul Alexander
Griefsong
POB 858
Amagansett, NJ 11930
(800) 538-4158
www.griefsong.com/meditationhealing.html

Notes

Preface

1. Mitch Albom, *Tuesdays with Morrie: An Old Man, a Younger Man, and Life's Greatest Lesson* (New York: Doubleday, 1997).
2. Randy Pausch with Jeffrey Zaslow, *The Last Lecture* (New York: Hyperion, 2008).
3. Elisabeth Kübler-Ross, *On Death and Dying* (New York: Touchstone, 1969)
4. Linda Pastan, "The Five Identities of Grief," in *Grief and the Healing Arts: Creativity as Therapy*, edited by Sandra L. Bertman (Amityville, N.Y.: Baywood Publishing Company, 1999), 2.

Introduction

1. Sigmund Freud, "Mourning and Melancholia," in J. Strachey ed. and trans., *The Standard Edition of the Complete Psychological Works of Sigmund Freud* (1917; London: Hogarth Press, 1959); Viktor E. Frankl,

Man's Search for Meaning (New York: Washington
Square Press, 1959).

2. Thomas Attig, *How We Grieve: Relearning the World*
(New York: Oxford University Press, 1996), 11–13.

Chapter 1

1. Ronnie Janoff-Bulman, *Shattered Assumptions:
Towards a New Psychology of Trauma* (New York: Free
Press, 1992), 6, 9, 11, 18.
2. Tom Welch, personal communication, 2005.
3. Fund-raising letter (Portland, Maine: Center for
Grieving Children, 2003).
4. Job 16:9 (New Revised Standard Version).
5. Robert A Neimeyer, ed., *Meaning Reconstruction &
the Experience of Loss* (Washington, D.C.: American
Psychological Association, 2000), 4.
6. I have paraphrased here ideas from many of Neimeyer's
writings.
7. Harold S. Kushner, *When Bad Things Happen to Good
People* (New York: Avon Books, 1981), 46.
8. Dorothee Soelle, *Suffering* (Philadelphia: Fortress
Press, 1975), 138.
9. Pesach Krauss and Morrie Goldfischer, *Why Me?
Coping with Grief, Loss, and Change* (New York:
Bantam Books, 1990), 167.
10. Erik H. Erikson, *Childhood and Society* (New York:
W.W. Norton, 1950).
11. Ibid.
12. Gail Sheehy, *Passages: Predictable Crises of Adult Life*
(New York: E.P. Dutton, 1974).
13. Clea Simon, *Fatherless Women: How We Change after
We Lose Our Dads* (New York: Wiley, 2001), 22.

14. Therese Rando, *How to Go On Living When Someone You Love Dies* (New York: Bantam Books, 1988), 239.
15. Thomas Attig, *How We Grieve: Relearning the World* (New York: Oxford University Press, 1996).
16. Barbara Kingsolver, *Prodigal Summer* (New York: HarperCollins, 2000), 412.

Chapter 2

1. Joan Didion, *The Year of Magical Thinking* (New York: Knopf, 2005), 32.
2. William Bridges, *The Way of Transition: Embracing Life's Most Difficult Moments* (Cambridge, Mass.: Perseus Publishing, 2001), 219.
3. William Bridges, *Transitions: Making Sense of Life's Changes*, 2nd ed. (New York: Da Capo Press, 2004), 133.
4. *You Can Count on Me*, written and directed by Kenneth Lonergan (Hart-Sharp Entertainment, 2000).
5. Robert A. Neimeyer, Holly R. Prigerson, and Betty Davies, Criteria for Complicated Grief, in "Mourning and Meaning," in *American Behavioral Scientist* 46, no. 2 (2002). These criteria were proposed for inclusion in the fifth edition of the *Diagnostic and Statistical Manual of Mental Disorders*.
6. Quoted in Jane E. Brody, "Grieving When the Lost Are Never Found," *New York Times*, Sept. 25, 2001, Personal Health section.
7. From Neimeyer et al., "Mourning and Meaning," 242.
8. Kenneth Doka, ed., *Disenfranchised Grief: New Directions, Challenges, and Strategies for Practice* (Champaign, Ill.: Research Press, 2002), xiv.

9. Judith Guest, *Ordinary People* (New York: Penguin Books, 1976).
10. Claudia Black, *Changing Course: Healing from Loss, Abandonment and Fear*, 2nd ed. (Center City, Minn.: Hazelden, 1999), 9.
11. William Styron, *Darkness Visible: A Memoir of Madness* (New York: Random House, 1990), 79.
12. "Symptomatology and Management of Acute Grief," *American Journal of Psychiatry* 101 (1944): 141–48.
13. Elisabeth Kübler-Ross, *On Death and Dying* (New York: Simon & Schuster, 1969).

Chapter 3

1. Ronald D. Cohen, ed., *Alan Lomax: Selected Writings, 1934–1997* (New York: Routledge, 2003).
2. Jill Werman Harris, ed., *Remembrances and Celebrations: A Book of Eulogies, Elegies, Letters, and Epitaphs* (New York: Pantheon Books, 1999), xvii.
3. Ibid, 72.
4. www.lifegem.com; "Company Makes Gems From Loved Ones' Ashes," *Washington Post*, November 26, 2004.
5. Wendt Center for Loss and Healing, Washington, D.C., www.wendtcenter.org.
6. Clarissa Pinkola Estés, *The Creative Fire*, audiobook (Boulder, Colo.: Sounds True, 1991).
7. Anne Brener, *Mourning and Mitzvah: A Guided Journal for Walking the Mourner's Path through Grief to Healing* (Woodstock, Vt.: Jewish Lights Publishing, 1993).
8. Eileen McNamara, "Two Legacies in Blossom," *Boston Globe*, October 2, 2002.

9. John Bowlby, *Attachment and Loss*, 3 vols., (New York: Basic Books, 1973, 1980, 1999).

10. Dennis Klass, Phyllis Silverman, and Steven Nickman, *Continuing Bonds: New Understandings of Grief* (Philadelphia: Taylor & Francis, 1996).

11. Ibid.

12. Myrim Baram, *My Creations: In Memory of Our Son, Gabriel Baram* (Kibbutz Kfar Menahem, Israel: BBBrothers Press, 2001).

13. Myrim Baram, personal communication, February 3, 2002.

14. Isaiah 2:4 (New Revised Standard Version).

15. Baram, *My Creations*, 1.

16. Barbara D. Rosof, *The Worst Loss: How Families Heal from the Death of a Child* (New York: Henry Holt, 1999), 3.

17. Suzanne Laurent, "Her Family Will Never Be the Same," *Derry News*, Aug. 26, 1994, Living Arts section.

18. Rosof, *The Worst Loss*, 160.

19. Terry Martin and Kenneth Doka, *Men Don't Cry, Women Do: Transcending Gender Stereotypes of Grief* (Philadelphia: Taylor & Francis, 2000).

20. Monica McGoldrick, "The Legacy of Loss," in *Living Beyond Loss: Death in the Family*, edited by Froma Walsh and Monica McGoldrick (New York: W.W. Norton, 1991), 105.

Chapter 4

1. Michael Ryan, "She Found a New Family to Love," *Boston Sunday Globe*, *Parade* magazine, July 15, 2001, 4–6.

2. Ibid, 5.

3. Ibid, 5.

4. Neil Chethik, *FatherLoss: How Sons of All Ages Come to Terms with the Deaths of Their Dads* (New York: Hyperion, 2001), 41.

5. Ibid, 254.

6. Ibid, 41.

7. Victoria Secunda, *Losing Your Parents, Finding Your Self: The Defining Turning Point of Adult Life* (New York: Hyperion, 2000), xvi.

8. William Worden, *Grief Counseling and Grief Therapy* (New York: Springer Publishing, 2002), 38.

9. Phyllis Rolfe Silverman, *Never Too Young to Know* (New York: Oxford University Press, 2000), 58.

10. Worden, *Grief Counseling,* 37–45.

11. Therese Rando, *How to Go on Living When Someone You Love Dies* (New York: Bantam Books, 1988), 239.

12. Judith Guest, *Ordinary People* (New York: Penguin Books, 1976), 252.

Chapter 5

1. Bertolt Brecht (1898–1956), German communist and playwright, *The Mother* (1932; New York: Grove Press, 1994).

2. "John Walsh," *America's Most Wanted* Web site, www .amw.com/about_amw/john_walsh.cfm.

3. Lybi Ma, "The Making of an Activist," *Psychology Today,* May-June 2003, 28–32.

4. Ibid, 32.

5. Ibid, 30–32.

6. Darrell Scott with Steve Rabey, *Chain Reaction: Call to Compassionate Revolution* (Nashville: Thomas

Nelson, 2001), 63. Beth Nimmo and Scott have written *Rachel's Tears,* another book about Scott's remarkable daughter, Rachel Joy Scott, and her beliefs and writings. Further information can be found on the Web sites www.rachelschallenge.com and www.TheColumbineRedemption.com.

7. Hope Edelman, ed., *Letters from Motherless Daughters: Words of Courage, Grief, and Healing* (New York: Dell, 1995), xv. This book is a compilation of letters from women throughout the United States and Canada who requested more stories from other women after reading Edelman's *Motherless Daughters: The Legacy of Loss* (New York: Dell, 1994).

8. Claudia Black, *Changing Course: Healing from Loss, Abandonment, and Fear* (Center City, Minn.: MAC Publishing, 1999), 168.

9. Aaron Lazare, MD, *On Apology* (Oxford, U.K.: Oxford University Press, 2004), 231.

10. Desmond Tutu, interview by U Min Htet, BBCBurmese.com, Aug. 17, 2005, www.bbc.co.uk/myanmar.

11. Alan McIlhenny Jr, Center for Grieving Children, Annual Report 2000–2001.

12. Stephanie V. Siek, "Joined by Tragedy, Building for a Future," *Boston Globe,* May 25, 2006.

Chapter 6

1. John D. Morgan, "Toward a Definition of Spirituality," *The Forum Newsletter* (Association of Death Education and Counseling) 26, no. 2 (Mar.–Apr. 2000): 1–2.

2. Lama Surya Das, *Awakening to the Sacred: Creating a Spiritual Life from Scratch* (New York: Broadway Books, 1999), 9–10.

3. Harold S. Kushner, *When Bad Things Happen to Good People* (New York: Avon Books, 1981), 51–52.

4. Jane Brooks, *Midlife Orphan: Facing Life's Changes Now That Your Parents Are Gone* (New York: Berkley Books, 1999), 44–45.

5. Loren King, review of *Brother Born Again*, Boston Globe, May 27, 2001.

6. Ibid.

7. Ibid.

8. Ibid.

9. Anne Lamott, *Traveling Mercies: Some Thoughts on Faith* (New York: Anchor Books, 2000).

10. Donald B. Kraybill, Steven M. Nolt, and David L. Weaver-Zercher, *Amish Grace: How Forgiveness Transcended Tragedy* (San Francisco: Jossey-Bass, 2007).

11. Luke 6:37 (New Revised Standard Version).

12. Kraybill et al., *Amish Grace*.

13. Francesca Fremantle and Chögyam Trungpa, trans., *The Tibetan Book of the Dead* (Boston: Shambhala Publications, 1992). The title *Tibetan Book of the Dead* is misleading, because, according to many Buddhist teachers, its purpose is to show us how to live, to teach us the lessons of impermanence, and to help us understand and appreciate that death is a part of life.

Chapter 8

1. Robert A. Neimeyer, ed., *Meaning Reconstruction and the Experience of Loss* (Washington, D.C.: American Psychological Association, 2000).

2. Jerome Groopman, *The Anatomy of Hope* (New York: Random House, 2004), 26.

3. Viktor E. Frankl, *Man's Search for Meaning* (New York: Washington Square Press, 1959), 56.
4. Ibid, 56.
5. Helen Keller, *The World I Live In* (New York: The Century Co., 1908).
6. Groopman, *Anatomy of Hope*, 26.
7. John McAfee, *The Fabric of Self* (Woodland Park, Colo.: Woodland Publications, 2001), 135.

Chapter 9

1. Judith Viorst, *Necessary Losses* (New York: Fireside, 1986), 16–18.
2. Robert Neimeyer, *Lessons of Loss: A Guide to Coping* (Keystone Heights, Fla.: Psychoeducational Resources, 2000).
3. Joan Borysenko, *Fire in the Soul: A New Psychology of Spiritual Optimism* (New York: Warner Books, 1993), 49.
4. Ibid, 49.
5. Viktor Frankl, *Man's Search for Meaning* (New York: Washington Square Press, 1959), 11.
6. Borysenko, *Fire in the Soul*, 84.

Bibliography

Attig, Thomas. *How We Grieve: Relearning the World*. New York: Oxford University Press, 1996.

Bowlby, John. Attachment and Loss series. Vol. 3, *Loss: Sadness and Depression*. New York: Basic Books, 1980.

Cohen, Ronald D., ed. *Alan Lomax: Selected Writings, 1934–1997*. New York: Routledge, 2003.

Deits, Bob, *Life After Loss: A Practical Guide to Renewing Your Life After Experiencing a Major Loss*. Cambridge, Mass.: Lifelong Books, 2004.

Doka, Kenneth J., ed. *Disenfranchised Grief: New Directions, Challenges, and Strategies for Practice*. Champaign, Ill.: Research Press, 2002.

Erikson, Erik H. *Identity, Youth and Crisis*. New York: Norton, 1968.

Grollman, Earl A. *Living When a Loved One Has Died*. Boston: Beacon Press, 1977.

Harvey, John H., ed. *Perspectives on Loss: A Sourcebook*. Washington, D.C.: Taylor & Francis, 1998.

Klass, Dennis, Phyllis R. Silverman, and Steven L. Nickman, eds. *Continuing Bonds: New Understandings of Grief*. Philadelphia: Taylor & Francis, 1996.

Kübler-Ross, Elisabeth. *On Death and Dying*. New York: Simon & Schuster, 1969.

Janoff-Bulman, Ronnie. *Shattered Assumptions: Towards a New Psychology of Trauma*. New York: Free Press, 1992.

Martin, Terry L., and Kenneth J. Doka. *Men Don't Cry, Women Do: Transcending Gender Stereotypes of Grief*. Philadelphia: Taylor & Francis, 2000.

Neimeyer, Robert A., ed. *Meaning Reconstruction & the Experience of Loss*. Washington, D.C.: American Psychological Association, 2000.

Ring, Nancy C., Kathleen S. Nash, Mary N. MacDonald, Fred Glennon, and Jennifer A. Glancy. *Introduction to the Study of Religion*. Maryknoll, N.Y.: Orbis Books, 1998.

Sanders, Catherine M. *Grief: The Mourning After*. 2nd ed. New York: Wiley, 1999.

Silverman, Phyllis Rolfe. *Never Too Young to Know: Death in Children's Lives*. New York: Oxford University Press, 2000.

Stroebe, Margaret S., Wolfgang Stroebe, and Robert O. Hansson, eds. *Handbook of Bereavement: Theory, Research, and Intervention*. Cambridge, U.K.: Cambridge University Press, 1991.

Worden, J. William. *Grief Counseling and Grief Therapy: A Handbook for the Mental Health Practitioner*. 3rd ed. New York: Springer Publishing Company, 2002.

Index

Abernathy, Ralph D., 57–58
activist(s), xxi, 112, 175. *See
    also* identity type
    advantages, 130–31
    Berger as, 7
    description, 6, 116
    disadvantages, 131–32
    exploratory questions for,
        133–34
    finding balance, 132
    healing and growth strate-
        gies, 132–33
    helping others grieve and
        heal, 130
    outward and future orienta-
        tion, 112
    profiles of, 115–30
    reflections for, 134
    typical, 113–14
adolescent survivors, 45, 99
altruism, 114. *See also*
    activist(s)

Alzheimer's disease, 117, 118
"ambiguous loss," 31
America's Most Wanted (TV
    show), xxii, 113
Amish community, 154–55
*Amish Grace: How Forgive-
    ness Transcended Tragedy*
    (Kraybill et al.), 154–55
anger, 41, 43, 101
    at deceased, 32, 43–44, 101
    at God, 48
anticipatory grieving, case
    material of, 85–87, 104,
    122–23, 142–43, 148–49
attachment and loss, 64–66,
    137
attachment behavior, 64
Attig, Thomas, xxiii, 22

Baram, Myrim, 66–68, 174
bereaved. *See* survivor(s)

bereavement, 173. *See also specific topics*
Bible, 17, 19
Black, Claudia, 40, 125
Borysenko, Joan, 184, 185
Boss, Pauline, 31
Bowlby, John, 64–65
Brener, Anne, 60
Bridges, William, 26–27
"brief treatment" model, 50–51
Brinker, Nancy G., 62–63
Brooks, Jane, 144
Brother Born Again (film), 150–52
Buddha, 137
Buddhism, 136–37, 145–48

caregiver distress, 105
cases
    Amanda, 121–25
    Ann, 126–28
    Barry, 128–29
    Carl, 89–91
    Carol, 72
    Cheryl, 33–39, 47, 48
    Deidre, 40–45, 48
    Eileen, 174
    Elizabeth, 85–86
    Francaise, 73
    Helen, 152–53
    Jeanne, 97–99
    Josh, 145–48
    Linda, 145
    Marc, 150–52
    Martha, 86–87
    Miranda, 142–44
    Octavia, 87–88
    Paula, 148–50
    PJ, 99–105
    Rachel, 120–21
    Skip, 73–75
    Steve, 45–46
    Suzanne, 68–71
    Terry, 44, 47, 48
    Tina, 94–95
    William, 91–93
catastrophic stressors, 68
Center for Grieving Children, 127–28
charitable donations, creating a legacy through, 72–73
Chethik, Neil, 93–94
child, loss of, 68–72
child survivors, 47, 64–65, 93. *See also under* cases; parents
children
    response to death, 99, 127, 138, 146
    understanding of grief, 44–45
Christianity, 151
cognitions during acute grieving, 26
collective identity with other survivors, 114, 120

Columbine High School massacre, 118–19
commitment to self and others, making a, 51–53, 161. *See also* normalizer(s), profiles of
community. *See also* seeker(s), community/belonging; social support
forgiveness by entire, 155
compassion fatigue, 105
completion, sense of, 76–77
complicated grief, 33. *See also* survivor(s), who don't grieve
how normal grieving can become, 30–32, 105, 173
symptoms, 32
complicated mourning, 98
connectedness as antidote to grief, 185–86

death. *See also* grief/grieving; loss of loved one
belief in "something beyond," 155–56
denial of, xviii, 47, 48
factors that influence survivor's response to, 102 (*see also specific factors*)
making peace before, 86–87
delayed grief, 74–75, 91–93

denial. *See also* death, denial of
triggered by grief, 31, 40, 48
Didion, Joan, 25
disenfranchised grief, 35–37, 63, 144
Doka, Kenneth, 35–36, 75–76
dying process, survivors' experience of, 104–5

Edelman, Hope, 119–20
Erikson, Erik H., 8, 20
Estés, Clarissa Pinkola, 60
ethnic customs for honoring the dead, 59–61
eulogies, 57–58

families in which survivors do not grieve, 96–99
family reconciliation after a crisis, 94–95
fathers, loss of, 93–94, 123–24. *See also under* cases
fear, isolation, and connectedness, 185
forgiveness, 125–26, 142, 154–55. *See also* reconciliation
by entire community, 155
Four Noble Truths, 137
Frankl, Viktor, 153, 177–78, 184–85
Freud, Sigmund, 64–65

fundraisers as memorials,
72–73
future orientation, 112, 150–
52. *See also* hope

gardens as memorials,
61–64
gender differences in grieving,
75–76
God, 139–41, 156. *See also*
Bible; religion; seeker(s)
anger at, 48
grief counselor, becoming a,
126–28
grief/grieving, 173. *See also* loss
of loved one; survivor(s);
specific topics
belief that it is a short-term
process, 49–50
how it can reverberate
throughout one's life,
46–47
how the dying process influences, 104–5
as individualized, unpredictable, nonlinear process,
50, 89, 107–8, 168
nature of, 27
normal course of, 27–28
reappearance, 45–46
stages of, 50
symptoms of acute, 26
ways of healing, 169–70
grievers, types of, 75–76. *See*

also identity type; *specific
types*
Groopman, Jerome, 177,
179
Guest, Judith. *See Ordinary
People*
guilt, 96, 105. *See also* survivor
guilt

Harris, Jill Werman, 57
Healing Garden, 61–62
"holding on," 65
Holocaust survivors, 97, 107,
177–78. *See also* Frankl
hope, 172
grief as doorway to, 22–24
surviving and thriving by
finding, 177–82

"I Never Said Goodbye"
(song), 76–77
identity
determining who you are
now, 170–71, 179–80
finding/developing new,
174–75, 179–81 (*see also*
nomad(s))
four pillars of, 10–17,
163–67
how it changes from loss,
20–22
from old identity to new,
3–5

using meaning-making to discover new, 176–77
identity crisis, 20–21
"identity hang-ups," 169
identity type(s), xx–xxi, 4–5, 171
    description, xxi, 5–7
    determining one's, 162–70
    impact of loss and, 7
    pillars of identity and, 11–17
illness, lingering. See anticipatory grieving
instrumental grievers, 75–76
intuitive grievers, 75
Irish rituals and customs, 60–61
isolation, xviii, 80, 123, 152–53
    as core of fear, 185

Jahan, Shah, 62
Janoff-Bulman, Ronnie, 8
Jewish rituals and customs, 60. See also Baram, Myrim
Judaism, 139–40, 151

King, Martin Luther, Jr., 57–58
Kingsolver, Barbara, 23–24
Kottler, Jeffrey, 114
Krauss, Pesach, 19
Kraybill, Donald B., 154
Kübler-Ross, Elisabeth, 50–51
Kushner, Harold, 19, 140–41

Lamott, Anne, 154
Landy, Karen, 140
Laurent, Suzanne, 68–71
Lazare, Aaron, 125
"letting go," 65, 97, 156
Lindemann, Erich, 50–51
Lloyd, Rosemary, 139–40
Lomax, Alan, 57
Lonergan, Kenneth. See You Can Count on Me
loss of loved one. See also grief/grieving; survivor(s); specific topics
    affects everyone, xxii
    Berger's experience, xvii–xix, 1–3, 9–10, 22–23, 120–21
    and grieving process, 27–28
    hidden gifts of loss, 184
    long-term impact, 174
    multiple losses, 99–102, 128–29
    short-term impact, 173
    sudden/untimely, 30

magical thinking, 42, 43
Mandela, Nelson, 126
Martin, Terry, 75–76
Mashek, Debra, 114
McAfee, John, 179–80
McGoldrick, Monica, 78–79
McNamara, Eileen, 61
meaning. See also seeker(s)

meaning (*continued*)
  created from loss, 17–20
  search for purpose and,
    138–39
meaning-making used to
  discover new identity,
  176–77
memorial activities
  across cultures, 56, 59–61
  examples of, 58–62
memorialist(s), xxi, 56–58,
    175. *See also* identity type
  advantages, 77–78
  description, 5
  exploratory questions for,
    81–82
  healing and growth strate-
    gies, 79–81
  potential disadvantages,
    78–79
  profiles of, 66–77
  reflections for, 82
  typical, 62–66
Mexican rituals and customs,
  59–60
Midlife Orphan (Brooks), 144
Morgan, John D., 137–38
mortality
  confronting one's own, 3–4
  sense of own, 11–13, 142–
    43, 164
Motherless Daughters (Edelman), 119–20
mourning. *See also* grief/
  grieving

mediators of, 102
Mumtaz Mahal, 62

nature, connecting with, 145
Neimeyer, Robert, 8, 18, 176
"neutral zone" (stage in grieving), 27
9/11. *See* September 11, 2001
  terrorist attacks
Nolt, Steven M., 154
nomad(s), xxi. *See also* identity
  type
  all survivors begin as, 25
  apparent advantages, 47–48
  child survivors as more likely
    to become, 47
  description, 5
  disadvantages and problems,
    43–44, 48–51
  essence, 28–30
  exploratory questions for,
    53–54
  healing and growth strate-
    gies, 51–53
  other types reverting to
    behaving like, 46–47
  profiles of, 33–47
  reasons for being stuck in
    grieving process, 31–32
  reflections for, 55
  when acute grief leads to a
    long-term, 30–32
normalizer(s), xxi, 83, 175. *See
  also* identity type

advantages, 105–6
categories of, 83
description, 6
disadvantages, 106–8
exploratory questions for,
    109–11
healing and growth strate-
    gies, 108–10
profiles of, 85–105
recreating the family life
    they lost in childhood,
    89–91
reflections for, 111
typical, 84–85
Nucci, Georgia, 84–85

On Death and Dying (Kübler-
    Ross), 50
order vs. chaos, 140–41
Ordinary People (Guest),
    37–38, 107–8

parents
    children bonding with,
        64–65
    death affects each child dif-
        ferently, 151–52
photography, memorial, 58
Pimsleur, Julia, 151–52
professional help, types of,
    170
public rituals. *See* rituals
public tragedies. *See also*

September 11, 2001 ter-
    rorist attacks
    special concerns created by,
        39
purpose. *See* meaning

Q'ero Indians, 150

rage. *See* anger
Rando, Therese, 21–22, 106
"rebound marriages," 109
reciprocal altruism, 114
reconciliation. *See also* family
    reconciliation after a crisis
    before death, 85–87, 94–95,
        124–26, 152
relationship to the world,
    15–17, 167
relationships, toxic, 97–99
"relearning the world," xxii–
    xxiii, 22
religion. *See also* Bible; God;
    rituals; seeker(s); *specific
    religions*
    support from, 116, 139–43,
        155–56
repression, 97
risk taking, appropriate, 108
rituals, 59. *See also* memorial
    activities
    creating private, 70–71
    purposes, 68–69
    in various cultures, 59–61

role identity, 21. *See also* identity

Rosof, Barbara, 71–72

Scott, Darrell, 118–19

Scott, Rachel, 118–19

Secunda, Veronica, 96

security, 105

    loss of sense of, 16, 29, 48, 102–3

    sense of world as benevolent, 8

seeker(s), xxi, 135–36, 175. *See also* identity type

    advantages, 155–56

    belief in "something beyond" death, 155–56

    community/belonging, 153, 155–57

    description, 6–7

    disadvantages, 156–57

    exploratory questions for, 158–59

    healing and growth strategies, 157–58

    profiles of, 141–54

    reflections for, 159–60

    religion, spirituality, and, 139–41

    search for purpose and meaning, 138–39

    typical, 136–40

self. *See* identity

separation, 64–65

September 11, 2001 terrorist attacks, 32–34, 107. *See also* terrorism

case material, 94–95, 129, 131 (*see also* cases, Cheryl)

    Kenneth Doka on, 36

sharing personal stories, benefits of, 119–20

Sheehy, Gail, 21

sibling loss, 37–38

Silverman, Phyllis, 99

Simon, Clea, 21

social support, 52, 80, 153, 170. *See also* religion, support from

South Africa, 126

spirituality, 139–41, 156. *See also* God; religion; seeker(s)

Stepanek, Matthew, 177

stillbirths, 71–72

Styron, William, 46–47

suicide, 101–4

support groups, 52, 80. *See also* Center for Grieving Children

survivor guilt, 37–38, 101–2

survivor(s). *See also specific topics*

    changes in lives of, xix–xx, 3–4

    characteristics, xix–xx

    expecting to feel better quickly, 49–50

    identifying personal path to healing, 168

most daunting task facing,
xxii
need to "relearn the world,"
xxii–xxiii, 22
questions for, xviii–xix, 4, 10,
19–20, 22, 135, 181 (*see also
under specific identity types*)
tips for, 161–62
who don't grieve, 95–99
Surya Das, 138–39
Susan G. Komen for the Cure,
63
symbolic loss, 38–39

terrorism, deaths from, 33–34,
84–85, 94–95, 131. *See
also* September 11, 2001
terrorist attacks
time, sense of and orientation
toward, 13–15, 164–65
transition, 26–27
trust. *See also* security
learning to, 157
Tutu, Desmond, 125–26

unresolved grief, 33. *See
also* complicated grief;
nomad(s)

values and priorities, 165–67
changes in, 15
Victoria, Queen, 78–79
violent death, 59, 102,

154–55. *See also* Col-
umbine High School
massacre; terrorism
Viorst, Judith, 184

Walsh, Adam, xxii, 113–14
Walsh, John, xxii, 113–14
Weaver-Zercher, David L., 154
Web sites to commemorate
loved ones, 58
Welch, Tom, 9
Wendt Center for Loss and
Healing, 59
*When Bad Things Happen to
Good People* (Kushner),
140–41
Worden, William, 96–97, 102
worldview
changes to, 7–10, 163, 168
inward, 16–17
as means of understanding
self, 9–10
outward, 17, 112
writing, sustaining memory of
deceased person through,
68–71

You Can Count on Me (film),
28–30

Zen Buddhism, finding community and belonging in,
145–48

About the Author

Susan A. Berger, LICSW, EdD, founded The Center for Loss, Bereavement and Healing in Framingham, Massachusetts, where she has a clinical practice and offers workshops to professionals and hospices as well as general audiences. She has made numerous presentations on the five ways we grieve at professional organizations, including the Association for Death Education and Counseling and the National Association of Social Workers. Her article "Helping Survivors Find New Identity through an Innovative 'Identity Typology'" was published in *Resources in Education* (Greensboro: University of North Carolina, 2001). She has served as a hospice volunteer working with the dying and with bereaved families. She earned her doctorate in education from Harvard University as well as a master's degree in social work and a bachelor's degree in philosophy from Boston University. She also holds a certificate in thanatology from Mt. Ida College in Newton, Massachusetts.

Please contact Susan A. Berger through her Web site, http://susanaberger.com, to share your stories of how the death of your loved one influenced your life and your identity.